Maintain Balance in an Unsteady World

Experts Reveal Their Best Ideas, Insights, and Inspirations to Help You Enjoy a Life of Balance, Comfort and Happiness

Marley, Sometimes life deals us challenges that throws our life totally out of balance. It takes a lot of work, time, faith, prayer to balance that teeter totter we have in our lives. Hang in there! May it help to know that there are many people including me always praying for you! All the best. Ann Wright

Compiled by Doug Smart

James & Brookfield
J&B
Publishers

Maintain Balance in an Unsteady World

Managing Editor: Gayle Smart

Editor: Sara Kahan
Proofreader: Laura Johnson
Book Designer: Paula Chance

Disclaimer: This book is a compilation of ideas from numerous experts who have each contributed a chapter. As such, the views expressed in each chapter are those of the authors and not necessarily the views of James & Brookfield Publishers.

For more information, contact:
James & Brookfield Publishers
P.O. Box 768024
Roswell, GA 30076
✆ 770-587-9784

Library of Congress Catalog Number in Publication Data

ISBN: 0-9712851-1-X

10 9 8 7 6 5 4 3 2 1

TABLE OF CONTENTS

I Work, Therefore I Am

by Patti Wood, M.A., CSP

I have a friend who is a personal organizer. She used to work for a major broadcasting company — a job she landed right out of college. It was exciting, challenging and 80 hours a week. She had no friends outside of work and barely had the strength to grocery shop or do laundry on weekends. Then she was laid off.

"I didn't know I didn't have a real life," she said. "I was too numb to know. I thought I was living. Now I'm awake and trying to meet men to date and make friends. Actually, having a life is harder. It's much better but it's harder. My friends back at work are envious, but, like me, they wouldn't want to be out here unless they were forced."

For many American's work has become everything. It devours their time, their physical and mental energy, and now, for some, it's become their major relationship — what some researchers describe as the "new romance." Like my friend, you may not even know that work has taken over your life. You simply go back and forth from home to your job, up and down on the seesaw.

Americans are spending more time at work than we would have thought possible 20 years ago. After 100 years of increasingly shorter work weeks, our work week stabilized at 40 hours after World War II, according to Benjamin Hunnicutt, a professor of history at the University of Iowa. Now two out of three Americans work more than 40 hours a week and one in 12 works 60 or more hours a week.

How has this happened? A string of reasons: political maneuvering, social pressure, consumerism, longer work hours, and ego gratification.

Politics

As you may have always suspected, work is an evil government plot. Ever since the Depression, our government has realized that ensuring everybody works means a steady tax flow. Leisure time doesn't pay taxes. We actually choose government officials who promise us steady work. What are we thinking? Working increases taxes and the gross national product that the government loves to brag about; why wouldn't its officials want us to work more?

Peer Pressure

Peer pressure doesn't just affect teenagers who are choosing whether or not to take drugs, it also affects adults choosing how to live their lives. Work is the drug of choice among many Americans. Recently, I took my first vacation in a year. I found myself bragging to my clients and friends and even my airplane seatmate. Not that I was going on a vacation. But that I had denied myself even those few days of pleasure for more than a year. Essentially, I was saying, "Don't I deserve your praise for working so hard?" "Don't you think I am a good girl?" There is pleasure in denial. Have you ever found yourself telling your peers about your long work weeks and doing what I call the "fake brag" about working on weekends?

My friend Michael lives in Paris, and he says it's rude to ask people that you meet there what they do for a living. You are supposed to ask people what they do for fun and about their family. That is what's most important to them. Michael works very hard, but he is allowed two-hour lunches and vacations that are long enough to go to Corsica for a month. All that, and they serve those tasty Mediterranean olives with cocktails, too.

Consumerism

We owe, we owe, it's off to work we go. We have chosen to work for stuff. Owning stuff feels good. Going to the mall and buying something provides immediate gratification. We work longer hours to get the nicer car to commute to the job with the longer hours.

Purchasing stuff is actually viewed as a sign of entrance into adulthood. Being responsible and successful is defined as not just having a full time job, but owning lots of stuff and having a hundred credit cards to pay for all the stuff. Other cultures have a different idea of what it means to grow up. In Australia, taking a year off to travel is seen as an important rite of passage into adulthood.

Our president even tells us that shopping is patriotic. When we are attacked by terrorists and our soldiers are off fighting wars, he says, "Be a good American, go out and buy stuff." Buying red, white and blue napkins and flower pots is akin to saluting the flag.

For a long time my friends wondered why I kept my 300-dollar a month apartment for 11 years, my Honda Civic for nine years and watched a small black and white TV that I got back in graduate school. Why did I wait so long to buy a house and begin accumulating nice things? Because I absolutely loved my life the way it was.

I passionately love being a speaker, but I feared taking certain speaking jobs just in order to pay the bills. I feared getting addicted to stuff. Well, now I have a four-bedroom house, a nice car and a color TV, and like most of my friends, I am battling with the "luxury over the leisure" dilemma.

As I type this, I'm looking out my window at the landscaper that I'm working to pay so that I can have a nice view out of my office window while I am working. I would really like to take two weeks off to go to Paris, but I have that pesky house payment.

When my best friend was dying sixteen years ago, he started giving away his stuff. His nice furniture and nice clothes didn't mean a darn thing. He told me he wished we had gone to Paris together. As for his high-powered job . . . well, people from work didn't even come to the hospital on his first stay. A year of hospital stays later, there was only myself, one other friend, and his family by his bedside on the day he died. It was clear what really mattered.

Fear of Intimacy

Work and consumerism protect us from messy family closeness. Last Thanksgiving, I visited my family. Immediately upon my arrival, we all went shopping. Everyone else was shopping, too. First we shopped for more food, and then we shopped at the mall. Next, we went to the video store to rent a movie. None of my family members had to have a conversation with each other for three whole days. We said things like, *How does this look on me? Should I buy this? Yum, this turkey sandwich is good* and *Have you seen this movie yet?* We dared not have a spare moment when intimacy could creep in.

We are actually a close family, but stuff can keep us from getting too close. This past Christmas my extended family of ten spent five hours opening presents. My 21-year-old nephew, who works with school children and sings in a band on weekends said, "Next year let's give only two gifts to each person and not waste so much money. And we can spend Christmas together, maybe doing volunteer work, instead of shopping and wrapping presents." He is wise beyond his years.

For some, work has become an escape. Family life is a matter of keeping a good calendar, being a taxi service and outsourcing. We are too tired from work and commuting to be close to each other. Work becomes an escape from the boring tasks of family life. For singles, work can be an escape from the scary prospect of dating and the heartache of romantic relationships.

A colleague and I have been teaching a continuing education class at a local university for the past six years. The class is called the "Meeting of the Minds." It nurtures group discussions on many different issues. Whenever we have a class member from another country such as Australia, Germany, or Brazil, they talk about our addiction to work and to "stuff." They comment on our choice to work for stuff. They like our stores, but wonder why we would rather work than play.

One young woman from Australia was in the middle of a year-long holiday after having just finished school, and she said, "My family doesn't have a washing machine, or two cars, but we all eat together and neighbors come over and visit just about every night. It's a good life. I feel lonely here. Everyone works late and then they are so tired from working, that they 'veg' in front of their television sets. That makes no sense. When do you live?"

Longer Work Hours

It's pretty basic. Wherever you spend the most time becomes the most important aspect of your life. If you're working 12-hour days, your personal identity, your community, your friends and your life's meaning have to come from work. Work is our new religion. We pray not to keep God in our lives, but to keep our jobs and paychecks. Cutback and layoffs have made us terrified of *not* working all the time. Perhaps the prospect of a hole in your life where your big job and or big paycheck used to be should give you the opportunity to fill that hole with something more important.

I recently read that in Norway, government officials can be called in to investigate complaints about employees being forced to do repetitive work or to work at too fast a pace. Can you imagine that in the United States? No one would even think of complaining!

The New Romance

This devotion to work affects our relationships. If we are spending more time at work, then it becomes more important. We must justify our sacrifice. Because we sacrifice other relationships to be at work, it becomes our major relationship. And it's not just a tryst for men. As the number of women entering the workforce continues to increase, many of them have traded "My husband's job defines me," to "My job defines me and I don't have to pick up my job's socks." Work is an *easy* date.

There is a trend for Americans, on average, to move every five years. Church attendance is down significantly, everyone knows the divorce rate is high, and we put the old parents in nursing homes instead of the downstairs bedroom as the Waltons did. Our one constant is work. You can always depend on work. There's a TV ad in which a young guy in a T-shirt gets his new business cards. He looks at the card as if it's a beautiful woman, and then he kisses it. Face it, we are dating our jobs.

And when the "relationship" doesn't go well, we freak out. There is nothing to balance the loss. Where will you find love in the workplace besides an office affair? The love of ego gratification fills up our hearts. When you work hard, you get praise. If this gratification isn't there or if we are having problems at work, even if we have spouses and children, recent research says we feel destroyed. Psychologists say our emotional responses to work problems and layoffs have become eerily similar to the way we used to react to divorce or the death of a loved one.

In the book *The Superman Complex*, Max Carey demonstrates how seeking success keeps us from getting close to each other and our true selves. When people exhibit Superman traits they believe they can do anything well, they are always right, they can work nonstop, and they don't need anyone. While those qualities may not be applicable of everyone, they clearly show what we value.

I think about my own life. After 20 years as a speaker, researcher and writer, I am now being recognized nationally as a body language expert. I get calls from magazines like *US Weekly*, *Cosmopolitan*, and *In Touch* wanting my expertise about nonverbal communication. I fly to New York and California to be on national TV shows. National news shows like "Dateline" and "FOX News" want my opinions and reads on celebrities and politicians. It is incredible fun, something I worked very hard to achieve, but added to my speaking, research and writing, means work is taking up all my life. Today I had to apologize to two of my best friends for not returning their phone calls for a week, my sweetie keeps saying I look tired, and my dog keeps bringing me her leash hoping for a long walk like we use to take.

I think it's time to rethink this work thing. In fact, I think I'm done writing for the day. I am going call my friends and invite them to dinner, call Delta Frequent Flyer Miles program and book a flight to Paris for this summer, and then I'm going to plant a few flowers in my own yard and have lunch. I might even have lunch with my boyfriend who, unlike my job (or my business card), can kiss me back.

ABOUT PATTI WOOD, M.A., CSP

Patti Wood, M.A.,CSP is an international speaker and trainer. Since 1982 she has designed and conducted keynote speeches, workshops and convention seminars for hundreds of top companies and national associations. Clients include: AT&T, GTE, Chick-fil-A, Dupont, Elli Lilly, Merck Pharmaceuticals, Lucent Technologies, The Kroger Company, Nortel Networks, Price Waterhouse, Nextel, Hewlett Packard, and hundreds more. Clients describe her as a dynamic, high-energy, powerhouse presenter. Patti develops high-energy information-packed programs and laughter-filled relationships with participants that leave them talking in the halls about what they've learned. Patti has been researching, writing and speaking on nonverbal communication for more than 20 years, and has taught communication at the university level for 11 years. She is interviewed frequently by the media, including CBS and ABC radio news, the BBC, PBS, The Discovery Channel, Entrepreneur Magazine, Woman's World, The Washington Post, Cosmopolitan, The National Examiner, YM J-14, First for Women, *and* Expert Magazine *as a body language expert.* Time Magazine *recognized her nonverbal communication course at Florida State University as one of the top college courses in the country. She is a communication consultant for* US Weekly *and has written seven books and co-authored four. Her research on nonverbal communication led to her position as the National Spokesperson for Wrigley's Spearmint gum.*

Contact Information:
Patti Wood, M.A., CSP
2312 Hunting Valley Drive
Decatur, GA 30033
Phone: (404) 371-8228
E-mail: Pattiwood@PattiWood.com
Website: www.PattiWood.com
www.TheBodyLanguageLady.com

Life Happens

by Alan Boyer

Although I am a somewhat organized person and plan everything for my business, I woke up one morning to the realization that I had been just letting life happen, my personal life anyway. I discovered that I had spent time planning everything but my own life. The chances are slim of getting what you want by waiting for things to happen. Life doesn't just happen the way you want it. Designing your future, an exciting future — the one you want — and then acting to make it happen, is the only way to get what you want.

I believe many people want to provide a good living and luxuries for their families but end up at the end of their careers or of their lives discovering they got there at the expense of their families. While life was happening they had lost sight of their real goals. They were so busy being successful at work that they had lost sight of the goals for their personal lives. The rest of their lives were just happening while they worked hard on the job.

I believe that many people have vague goals for their life, but have not planned how to get there. They are waiting for life to happen rather than taking control and making it happen.

Do you see others around you that appear to be lucky, good

things happening to them, while you seem never to have any luck? Then create the future you want, a future that is balanced across all of the areas of life. Don't wait for luck to find you — it isn't likely that it will without help from you.

Decide now to create your own future — not just any future, but an extraordinary future. Decide that you will do everything extraordinarily better than you have in the past.

Steps for creating a future which includes all areas of life important to you:

1) Change the behaviors and attitudes that are keeping you where you are.
2) Learn from those who are succeeding.
3) Look inside yourself to see what really matters.
4) Identify and overcome the obstacles.
5) Set clear goals (the right goals, the right way).
6) Develop a plan and vision (a powerful one).
7) Make it happen (don't wait for life to happen).

All seven steps are important to creating your future; however, the most important, and probably the most difficult on that list, is changing behaviors and attitudes. The other six won't be successful until the first has happened. If you expect different results from those you've previously had, you must change what you have been doing. You have to change your behavior (how you have acted) and change your attitude (how you look at yourself and your surroundings).

If you think what you've always thought
then you will feel the way you've always felt.
If you feel the way you've always felt
then you'll do what you've always done.
If you do what you've always done
then you'll get what you've always gotten.
If you get what you've always gotten
then you'll think what you've always thought.

— Anonymous

Your success will come from looking into yourself to discover the new ways of thinking, feeling, behaving, responding, and then taking charge to make it happen, not wait for life to happen.

1) Changing behaviors and attitudes

Behaviors

Ask yourself if you have achieved the success you want. As long as you continue doing what you have been doing, you are going to continue to get what you have been getting. What behaviors have to change if you expect a different outcome? If you have already been successful, then you are doing the right things, but if you haven't seen success, or at least the level of success you desire, then you have to change a behavior.

Behaviors and attitudes go together. How you feel about something often results in a behavior or a lack of behavior. Unsuccessful people let their feelings determine their behavior. Successful people know that their behavior determines their feelings. Their good feelings come from their successes.

Right behaviors

- Take responsibility for everything that happens in your life.
- Take action to make your life what you want it to be. Don't wait for life to happen. Create it.
- Never say can't. Turn a "can't" into a "can do."
- Clearly identify what you want to happen.
- Plan and act.

Attitudes

Change from this attitude:

- Can't — Can't — Can't — Been there, done that. It won't work this time either.
- Victim — My business is not doing well because of the economy *or . . .*
- After something went terribly wrong you hear someone say "it wasn't my fault; it was the other guy's fault."

To this attitude:

- Always look for a way to make it happen.
- You are not at the mercy of anything or anyone. Find a way to fix it, no matter what. You either choose to fix it or be a victim.

Let's examine how we often think. We typically take all of our input data and funnel it through our paradigms and all of our "can'ts." In most cases we get less than 10 percent of the original information through to work with.

Most decisions are made without having all of the facts. We've filtered out and thrown away 90 percent of the available information.

So how do we improve on that?

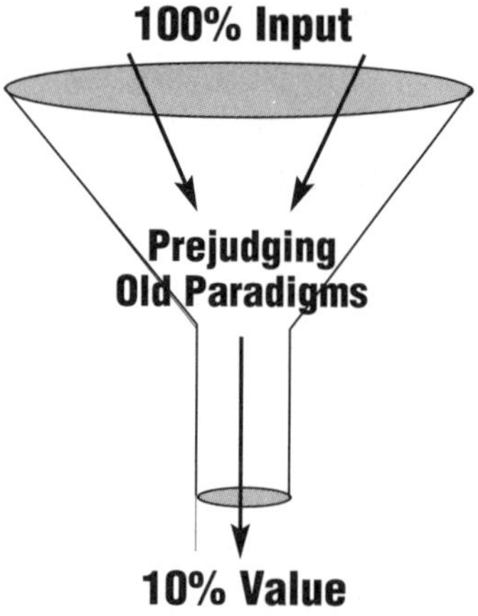

Turn the funnel upside down and take another look.

The next time someone says, "something can't be done," even if that someone is you, stop and think of a way to make it work. Now you are adding some creative thought rather than throwing out ideas. You get 100 percent plus the added value, the creative value that you can add to all of your available data.

Build a list of all of the ways that you can make life happen. You can add that to all of the other ideas that will be coming in, then prioritize among the best. Now you have a lot more ideas, and creative ones at that.

Be aware whenever you are saying, "It can't be done." STOP . . . turn your funnel upside down.

"Some look at things that are, and ask why.
I dream of things that never were and ask why not?"
— George Bernard Shaw

We view a problem either as an obstacle or a wall. If we view a problem as a wall with no way around, then we have chosen not to look for a way around it. An obstacle has a way around it; we just have to find it.

Victimization — Becoming a victim is a choice. I usually hear a stirring in the crowd when I say that. Some are sure that they couldn't help what happened to them. When something happens to us that seems to be out of our control, we have to decide what we will do about it rather than just let it happen. We also have to look at why we sometimes just let things happen to us. Yes, I said *we let things happen to us.* Take responsibility for everything that happens and you will suddenly be in control.

What happens when we say we are at the mercy of something or someone? We have given up because we view life as out of our control. However, if we decide that we have control of everything that happens in our life then we just have to find the obstacle and the path around it.

When one of my clients talks about how the economy has hurt his business, he has chosen to be a victim of the economy rather than looking for a way to work around that obstacle. I ask him how much of the market he has. The answer usually is, if he even knows, well less than one percent. So I ask him, "If there is 99 percent of the market still out there buying, why does the other fellow have it and not you?" Now, instead of living with a small part of the market that is declining, he starts looking for ways to get a bigger piece of the market, and he does it. It's a decision to be a victim and stop trying before exploring the options or to think out of the box. Deciding to act or not act is your choice.

We cannot keep doing the things we have been doing or thinking the way we've been thinking. If we haven't already discovered success, then we must look deeper inside ourselves and change what we have been doing. Some thought patterns must change.

"A great many people think they are thinking
when they are merely rearranging their prejudices."
— William James

2) Learn from those who are succeeding

The fastest way to get ahead is to learn from those who are already doing it. Ask those who are succeeding what they are doing. Implement those strategies that fit your goals.

3) Look inside yourself

Align short-term goals with long-term life goals. Look for a balance between all of the key elements of your life, both personal and business. I believe that true success and happiness come from having a balance in life and achieving not only business goals but also the important personal life goals.

Personal

Organizational

What is really important to you?

Look inside yourself to know who you are and what you really want. I believe that we all have superficial desires and some really deep down desires. However, because some of the deep down desires haven't been verbalized or seriously thought through, we sometimes don't even know what they are or that some of our superficial desires may be contradictory.

Finding a balance for life is what is needed. Instead of focusing hard on one area of life, focus on all areas to see how success in all areas is better than success in one.

Take a look at the two wheels on page 18. Assume that the center of the wheel represents zero progress toward where you want to be, and the outside rim equals 100 percent of where you'd like to be. Place a mark at that level you feel you have accomplished for each of the six areas on the personal wheel and each of the four areas on the organizational wheel.

Then ask yourself if you removed the outer rim of the wheel, if this wheel would roll along smoothly. Would it be a rough ride? If so, is that ride an indication of what your life has been like?

Write at least two goals for each of the categories in each wheel. They can be new goals, or they can be existing goals. If they are existing goals, enter the percentage toward your goal you have achieved so far.

Personal	%	**Organizational**	%
1) Financial		1) People skills	
____________________	_____	____________________	_____
____________________	_____	____________________	_____
2) Mental		2) Sales/influencing skills	
____________________	_____	____________________	_____
____________________	_____	____________________	_____
3) Physical		3) Productivity	
____________________	_____	____________________	_____
____________________	_____	____________________	_____

4) Social %

____________________ _____

____________________ _____

5) Spiritual

____________________ _____

____________________ _____

6) Family

____________________ _____

____________________ _____

4) Time Management %

____________________ _____

____________________ _____

Now develop a plan to achieve balance in that wheel, to achieve the goals in each area of your life.

4) Identifying and overcoming the obstacles

Asking yourself some questions will help you identify what has to happen in order to change and take charge of your life and success.

- If the goals you have written are so important, why haven't they already happened?
- What has stopped you from achieving those goals?

These are the obstacles that must be identified and removed.

- What has it cost in money, relationships, and time because you haven't achieved some goals already?
- How much benefit will you receive if you choose to remove those obstacles?

One of the attitudes I wrote about earlier was "can" versus "can't." There is always a way around an obstacle as long as you don't think of it as a wall.

I often hear clients tell me that people should be positive, so they wonder why I am looking at the obstacles, what they consider as negatives. I emphasize that one of the keys to achieving success is to identify the obstacles that have been in our way so they can be removed. To continue doing the same things we have been doing with less than desired results is getting negative results. To look at the obstacles and remove them or find a way around them is a positive behavior.

From this day forward, whenever you have something that is important to you, ask yourself:

- If this is so important to me, why hasn't it already happened?
- What are the obstacles between me and my goals?

Then find a way around the obstacles and start again.

5) Goal setting (doing it the right way)

a) Write the goals.
b) Define the benefits of achieving them and the consequences of standing still.
c) Goals must be SMART.
d) Goals must be results oriented, not activity oriented.
e) Act on the goals.

Writing your goals down is key to your success. A goal that is not written is vague and often does not get done. The simple act of writing something locks it in your mind. Additionally, something written is a physical object that can be looked at, adjusted, fixed and optimized.

Having written goals and plans gives you an object that you can hold and fix. When I worked as an engineer, I often thought through a design in my head. It was easy to say, "no problem, that's easy." However, once it was written down I discovered that I saw so much more that I was forced to think through all of the intricacies. The projects were never as easy as I had originally thought they would be. When I looked at a written diagram or plan, the pieces started to solidify and come together. After that I started seeing new ways of implementing the plan, and it became better and more efficient. The same is true of written goals and life plans.

I believe that most of us have goals only in our heads. I often hear people say their goals are to be better next week, to lose weight next month. These are too vague. You can't hit what you can't clearly see or measure.

What happens to vague goals? They frequently are not achieved. Written goals tell us what our success should look like. If we don't even know what success looks like, how do we know when we get there? What is driving us to achieve these goals when they aren't even clear?

A goal should be SMART:

Specific
Measurable
Attainable
Reachable (but with a challenge)
Time-based

The goal to be better next week should change to look something like this:

Specific

Clearly defined what is to happen to what.

A clear goal — I want to increase my sales by $2,000. (It is specifically sales and by how much.)

A vague goal — I want to be better.

Measurable

We can measure our progress toward the goal, and measure success when we get there.

Measurable — Increasing sales by $2,000 is measurable. (We know exactly when we get there, and can measure our progress along the way.)

Not measurable — I want to be better.

By making our goals measurable, we can measure our progress toward our goals. Measuring our progress helps us see progress. Seeing progress keeps us motivated and excited. Having the measurement also gives us a tool to have control of our progress. When we aren't moving as well as we had hoped, we are aware that we have to make changes (there's that *change* word again) to get back on track. Seeing how much progress, or lack of progress we are making, and where we are in the timeframe causes us to drive harder to get back on track when we get behind.

If our goal is to increase sales by $2,000 a week, then by mid-week we'd like to see that we are halfway to the target. If we're not, then we have to work on the changes (that word again), either doing more or changing what we are doing.

If our goal is simply "to be better next week," what drives us? We don't even have a clear picture of what better is or when next week really comes.

Attainable

If goals are:

Attainable — Setting goals we know we can reach results in working harder to achieve them.

Not Attainable — Why try to hit them? We know we can't.

Goals that are continually set out of reach result in our knowing that we aren't going to be able to reach them.

Reachable (but with a challenge)

This is where we are challenged to reach farther than we have before. We get better by challenging ourselves to reach just a little farther than we did last time.

Time-based

Having a specific time target challenges us to hit that goal in time and drives us to work to hit the target as we see the goal line coming up.

- A target to increase sales by $2,000 by close of business on Friday is a visible goal. As we measure our progress and see that we have attained only $800 by Wednesday we know we either have to work harder or change what we are doing to increase our sales toward the Friday goal. By Thursday, we see the end coming and adjust accordingly.

> What happens when Friday comes and we are off by a couple of hundred dollars? If this was an important goal, then wouldn't we readjust, re-plan, change something, and work harder to make up that $200 next week? How can we do that if our goal is simply to be "better"?

The key to consistently achieving your goals is to ask yourself: Am I achieving my goals?

Yes
- What did I do right?
- Learn from it.

No
- Why not?
- What is the obstacle?
- Develop a plan to remove the obstacle.
- Try again.

Achieving goals gives us a feeling of confidence and we are likely to try even harder next time. If you are not achieving your goals on a regular basis, how does that make you feel?

What would it do for you to achieve your goals on a regular basis? Would you feel like a success? There's that attitude change we were looking for. The more you succeed, the more you are going to feel confident. The more confident you are, the more likely you are to succeed.

Results-based Goals vs. Action-based Goals

Goals that are focused on results rather than just on actions are more likely to be achieved. We lose sight of the real goal when we are focused only on actions. Always focus any goal or plan on results, not just actions.

An example might be that we want to see a sales increase of $2,000 and have made the assumption that we just have to make 100 more cold calls than last week to be able to do that. So, we set our goal to make 100 more cold calls this week. We make the 100 more calls and add only an extra $1,000. What went wrong? Do we get frustrated when we have achieved our action goal but didn't achieve the results we wanted?

Let's change our goal to increasing our sales by $2,000. Then we develop some action steps to achieve our goal, one of which is to make

100 more cold calls, another is to review the results of the cold calls at the end of each day and review other options. If we see that the cold calls are not working well, then we know that we must regroup and change the actions to hit our $2,000 goal.

By setting goals for the results rather than the actions, we are focused on doing whatever it takes to achieve the result rather than doing actions that might not achieve the goal and stopping there.

6) Planning

- Gives us a vision of what success looks like and how to get there.
- Keeps our goals focused on the end result of the bigger picture.
- Is where it all comes together in creating our future.

Having a vision, a picture of what your goals look like and what your life should look like, is what keeps us focused on the end results and the path along the way.

Personal

Visualize how you want to be seen at the end of your life, what you want to have accomplished. Then visualize your life, perhaps marriage and children (from babies to adulthood), and on through retirement. Consider how you want to be thought of by associates, friends, and family.

Business

Visualize what you would like your business (or job) to look like at retirement, in ten years, five years, one year, and the next six months. How do you want to be thought of by employees and customers?

Then build a plan to make it happen. Don't accept any can'ts along the way.

7) Making it happen

This is where the rubber meets the road.

You must take responsibility for what happens in your life.

- Create your extraordinary future.
- Create a better life for yourself.
- Create a better company.
- Create a better family.
- Create better relationships.
- Create a better world.
- Don't wait for life to happen. Act today to create the rest of your life.

You can improve the probabilities (put luck on your side) if you take these steps.

1) Change the behaviors and attitudes that are keeping you where you are.
2) Learn from those who are succeeding.
3) Look inside yourself to see what really matters.
4) Identify and overcome the obstacles.
5) Set clear goals (the right goals, the right way).
6) Develop a plan and vision (a powerful one).
7) Make it happen (don't wait for life to happen).

As a reminder to *Never Let Life Happen — Create Life the Way You Want It*, make a copy of the symbol at the top of the page and put it where you can see it every day.

ABOUT ALAN BOYER

Alan Boyer, President and founder of The Leaders Perspective, is an executive coach and personal coach, a Total Quality consultant, and professional speaker. He has made his mission in life to help everyone he meets to achieve their dreams and goals whether or not they are his clients. Many of his clients have experienced significant growth (some doubling their business) after starting with him.

More than 35 years experience as an electrical engineer, Vice President, and business/quality consulting in companies such as Sony Corporation of America, Lear Jet Stereo, 3-M, Sprint and many smaller companies throughout the U.S. and the Pacific Rim. In 2003 he became Vice President of Finance for the National Speakers Association. Alan was responsible for quality improvements for Sony Corporation of America, taking the U.S. Sony-owned manufacturing and the subcontractors from worst in the world to best in the world within two years, which is significant considering the Japanese philosophy for quality.

Contact Information:
Alan Boyer
The Leader's Perspective
6 Pemford Place
Liberty, MO 64068
Phone: (816) 916-6141
Fax: (816) 781-4312
E-mail: AlanBoyer@leaders-perspective.com
Website: www.leaders-perspective.com

DEFINING BALANCE

by Laurie Santulli

All too often, in this crazy world of voice mail, e-mail, cell phones and PDAs, we get caught up in the pressures and demands of everyday life, particularly our jobs, and lose sight of the fact that the hours and minutes we expend each day make up our lives. Sometimes we become numb to the fact that we are indeed living. This is your life! This is my life! And it is up to each of us individually to create it and live it according to our specific needs and purpose.

More often than not, it takes a tragic or profound event to wake us up to realize that perhaps this is not the life we originally intended to live or the life we want to die living. Although there are demands on our time and attention from the "shareholders" in our lives — bosses, employees, customers, spouses, children — it is ultimately up to us to define balance for ourselves. We are the CEOs of our lives, and we're responsible for setting into motion deliberate strategies, decisions and actions that will allow us to intentionally live the unique, balanced lives we envision.

Defining Balance

I define life balance as "bringing into harmony the physical, intellectual, emotional and spiritual needs of one's being."

Essentially, it's taking care of your whole self so you are better equipped to serve other people in your life. Balance is not the same for everyone. Because each individual's spirit is unique, balance is characterized differently for each of us depending on our desires, our beliefs, and our responsibilities. What is offered here is a framework that will guide you as you take a step back and examine your life and its relationship to balance or state of equilibrium.

The framework is composed of four elements vital for achieving balance:

Elements of Human Balance

Physical Food Shelter Safety Health	**Intellectual** Learning Challenge Growth Thoughts/Beliefs
Emotional (Feelings) Self-Respect vs. Self-Abuse	**Spiritual (Purpose)** Making a Difference Giving Back

We will explore each element in the following sections. Then we'll use a five-step process designed to help determine your unique needs within each element.

> *"Health or wealth? It's such an obvious choice that you wonder why so many people choose the wrong one."*
>
> — Richard Rybolt, author of *No Chairs Make For Short Meetings*

Physical Needs

Physical may be defined as *"of or relating to the body, material as opposed to mental or spiritual."* According to Abraham Maslow's Hierarchy of Needs, there are five levels of human needs (see diagram, page 31).

The first level, at the bottom, must be satisfied before the successive higher levels will be considered or achieved.

You will notice the first two levels are in the physical realm. Most Americans are pretty well assured they will have adequate food, water, air and shelter. And prior to September 11, 2001, we were relatively

Maslow's Hierarchy of Needs

Self-Actualization

Esteem, Value and Respect

Belongingness and Love

Safety from Danger of Threat

Water, Food, Air, Physical Health

assured of our general safety. While there is a constant threat of terrorism now, and there certainly are homeless and hungry people in our country, these concerns do not consume everyday life for most of us because our communities have measures in place to handle them.

The need that we have the opportunity to handle ourselves is our physical health. The problem is that we have boundless access to food and drink at any time and at almost every place. Because of this abundance, we sometimes take better care of our cars than we do our bodies. With our vehicles, we probably "gas up" only when needed, change the oil on a regular basis, tune up the engine, check the brakes and rotate the tires according to the manufacturer's maintenance schedule. If we don't, our safety could be on the line.

But what about our bodies? Sure, most of us regularly shower and shave and keep ourselves generally neat and clean, but do we really pay as much attention as we could to how we care for and maintain our bodies, the vehicles that give us life? Are we unaware, or is it just easier and seemingly cheaper to choose fast food over a more nutritious, beneficial choice? Are we simply so inundated by the constant surge of media messages about having to eat ("You gotta eat!"), eating on the run, "supersizing," and the like, that we give in and actually believe we have to eat what they tell us to, how they tell us to and how much they put on our plates?

In this environment, our animal instincts can emerge. For instance, no matter how much food is put in front of a dog, chances are the animal will eat it. My cocker spaniel will seek out food in briefcases, in the pantry, on the counter, in the trash — if there's food anywhere within her reach, she'll find it and eat it if she's not caught in time.

How many of you see yourselves in this description? I do. I was raised in a home with Depression-ingrained parents, and it was considered a sin to waste food. You were to eat what was on your plate no matter what. If I did that today, especially when eating out, I would easily be twice my size.

Professionals who care for their physical bodies on a consistent basis usually do so with a fervor. Nothing is going to get in the way of their workout, their time and their health if at all possible. They may have to reschedule and improvise, but they are committed. They seldom are found eating out of vending machines or the local candy jar. They understand they are primarily in control of their health and refuse to be a victim of circumstance.

If you're just getting started, you can increase your physical activity by parking farther away from your office building or the shopping mall (safety first, of course), climbing the stairs to your office or playing ball with your children after work.

When you're able to make it to a gym, review some memos or reports while you're on the exercise equipment. And if you have to, schedule workouts before your workday starts. Establishing this routine helps to make sure nothing interferes with this important personal time.

During a particularly stressful time, I remember being asked by my manager how I was doing. There had recently been a merger, lots of travel, competing and changing priorities, and way too much political maneuvering. My reply was, "I'm doing fine. I'm able to get my workouts in. They keep me sane." Along with the physical, there is a strong mental benefit to a regular exercise program.

"The wisest mind has something yet to learn."

— George Santayana (1863-1952)

Intellectual Needs

Intellectual, according to the dictionary, is defined as "*rational*" or "*given to study, reflection and speculation.*" Our society certainly supports formal education. But once our formal education is complete after high school, college, or trade school, what do we do to continue growing and expanding our minds? Learning, when we are young, can seem like a chore or even boring. But as we grow older we see it can be fun and, more importantly, very empowering.

You may have heard the phrase "continuous learning" in a business environment. Is it just a buzzword for you? Ask yourself whether you're being challenged intellectually. Are you learning something new? Are you updating your skills? Learning new approaches to your job? Opening your mind to see things from a different perspective? If not on the job, then in your personal life?

Finding yourself in a situation with little room for intellectual discovery can leave the mind stagnant — with stale thoughts, self-defeating attitudes and frustration. What about taking time to learn more about your hobbies — hunting, fishing, sewing, golfing, boating, gourmet cooking, refurbishing a car or motorcycle, birdwatching, studying philosophy, reading, or scrapbooking? Whatever it is you like to do or dream of doing, are you making time to discover how to do it or how to do it at the next level?

Or have you fallen prey to the "boob tube" mentality? After dinner, are you so worn out, you plop down in the cozy recliner and passively absorb the frequently negative images on TV, dutifully interspersed with those enticing food advertisements discussed previously? I had to ask myself this question as I recently sat on the couch watching Dr. Romano on "ER" get his arm cut off by a helicopter rotor. It was a gruesome scene. I knew it. I saw it the first time and here I was watching the rerun! Surely I had something more valuable to do.

Then, of course, there are the reality TV series, news programs, shows about murder, sexual assault, affairs, drug abuse, you name it. If it's an atrocity of our society, you can find it on TV. We also have newspaper headlines, radio programs and pop-up ads on the Internet delivering additional, mostly negative, messages into our precious minds and the minds of our children.

Where does this stop? First, we must assess the avenues whereby we take in communication and evaluate the communication delivered. Are they really the messages you want to be seeing, listening to and persuaded by? Are they providing positive value to your life or serving to make you depressed, agitated or just plain numb? And how much of your precious time is this constant glut of communication taking from other, more important areas of your life?

Instead of flipping through TV channels at night until you find something to capture your attention, why not consider doing something to fulfill your goals or dreams. Do you want to be a positive influence on your children's lives? Play a board game or the card game "Concentration" to help stimulate their minds and make them better students. Or play with your elderly parents to keep their minds sharp. Do you want to plant a beautiful garden in the spring? Why not read up on some gardening tips for new ideas. Are you dreaming about a big vacation? Why not start researching interesting destinations to visit and places to stay? Achieving balance is about intentionally living your life — the life you want, not the life food manufacturers, network TV, the media and society would like for you to live.

When I was 17, I let my mother's opinion of weightlifting stifle a dream of competing in a bodybuilding show. Fortunately, for me, that dream was revived, and I was able to envision the competition in my mind and then take it to fruition. It was the power of my mind that first made the competition seemingly impossible at 17 and then incredibly possible in my 30s. Once committed, I focused on what I could do to reach my goal, not on the obstacles that stood in the way. There was only one goal — a single-minded goal — to be the best I could be on stage in the contest and therefore only one choice — *no* choice but to follow the prescribed plan for success. That's discipline and that's the power of the mind — your mind. Please be careful what you're feeding it.

"I write entirely to find out what I'm thinking, what I'm looking at, what I see and what it means, what I want and what I fear."
— Joan Didion

Emotional Needs

Emotion is *"intense feeling (as of love, hate, or despair)."* A fine definition, except my intellectual mind wants to know, "What exactly is a feeling?" The word "feeling" is defined as *"the sense of touch, a state of mind, general emotional condition, sentiment, capacity to respond emotionally."*

Not completely satisfied with this definition either, I researched it further and found that I am not alone. As it turns out, hundreds of philosophers and researchers have tried to define emotion or feeling and have come up with hundreds of theories.

The best definition of emotion I have found, one that makes sense to my intellect, is that of Tom Rusk, M.D., in his book *Get Out of Your Own Way*. According to Dr. Rusk, "There can be no practical, in-depth understanding of feelings until you come to grips with the human spirit." Dr. Rusk teaches that emotions are the "language of the spirit" and the spirit "messages in the form of feelings and bodily sensations (such as muscle tension, digestive problems, headaches, blushing of the cheeks, quickening of the heart…)." So emotions are the language of our unique, individual spirits.

Assuming this definition has some truth to it, and I believe it does, it is critical that we learn to acknowledge and listen to our emotions and determine what they are telling us about a given situation. It is the only way to be true to ourselves, to be true to our inner spirit.

But how do we do this when we have limited time, are constantly bombarded with media messages, or have become insensitive to what we feel because we've been living our lives for other people or it's too painful to feel? And what about the fact that emotions are particularly shunned in a business environment?

The bottom line is we must make time. Again, this is about finding our own unique balance in life, and how is that possible if we can't make time to listen to what's going on inside of us, inside of our individual bodies? As for business stresses and addressing the challenge of emotions not being welcome in the workplace, the tendency is to stifle and stuff our true feelings. And when we aren't able to or don't express our emotions, they can manifest themselves as muscle tension, stiffness, ulcers, disease and/or anger. This is certainly not the prescription for balance, health or vitality.

For me, in retrospect, it's clear that I was living my life based on the expectations of others, including society in general. My spirit wanted to do a bodybuilding competition when I was younger, but I didn't listen to my heart. I studied engineering because I thought it would be marketable and bring me a top-dollar salary. I worked innumerable hours because I thought it was expected of me.

But what about me? What about the desires of my spirit? I became so wrapped up in my work, I lost all perspective on life, became ill, and seldom, according to my boss, even smiled. Surely my life would have been different had I been discerning enough to listen to my emotions before I was in my 30s.

But I can't change the past and neither can you. We can, however, create change for a brighter, more satisfying future.

What is important here is that we take time to listen to our inner voices and the sensations of our bodies, since our emotions do manifest themselves within our bodily tissues. Sometimes these manifestations become so comfortable and familiar to us we can't recognize them, and subsequently we are unable to acknowledge and interpret them.

So find a few minutes of quiet time each day. Turn off the radio in the car on your way to work, sit on your porch in silence, bypass TV for a night, take a walk during a break from work and become in tune with your emotions and what they are trying to tell you.

If there are work stresses that are weighing heavy on your spirit, find a healthy way to express those feelings. Use journaling, sharing with a confidante, or a private conversation with your boss. Even if you don't get the outcome you desire, you will have dealt with a stressful circumstance, articulated your concerns and enabled yourself to breathe a little easier.

Another suggestion is to lie quietly and still on a lounge chair, or before you go to sleep at night, reflect on the occurrences of your day and notice the sensations your body experiences. Do you feel muscle tightness, tension? Are you smiling? Frowning? Are you sad? Do you desire comfort? Can you remember what you dreamed about doing when you were a child? Have you accomplished it, or is it something you'd still like to do? Is thinking about it making you feel eager? Hopeful? Happy?

Depending on your introspection and responses, determine which situations, dreams or desires you want to address and evaluate what you can actually do to make them happen. Or in the case of stressors, determine what you can possibly do to alleviate them. Pay attention to your inner voice as you make your decisions to determine which will give your spirit a sense of self-respect and which will diminish it.

One needs something to believe in, something for which one can have whole-hearted enthusiasm. One needs to feel that one's life has meaning, that one is needed in this world.
— Hannah Senesh

Spiritual Needs

Spirit is defined as *"life-giving force, soul, disposition, mood, the essence of real meaning."* Religious discussions are definitely taboo in most business environments. But, as I learned on my journey, religion does not necessarily make one spiritual. Attending weekly services, as I did most of my life, doesn't guarantee spiritual awareness.

It's important to make sure what you're doing with your business and personal life aligns with your spiritual values and purpose. Being raised Catholic, I was taught that going to church regularly was mandatory. If you didn't, you were going to Hell. Somehow that didn't put me more in touch with my spirituality. It only made me fearful.

This strict religious upbringing also taught me to believe that I could and should achieve perfection. I expected it not only of myself but also of those around me. Then one day, a trusted confidante said to me, "Laurie, there's no such thing as perfection." I wasn't sure I had heard her right. I was shocked, stunned, in disbelief. I had spent 30-something years striving for and falling short of perfection (getting darned close though, I thought), and now I was confronted with the stark realization that I had been striving for the impossible, the unattainable.

It was only after digesting this reality intellectually and emotionally that I was free to even consider accepting myself as I was and now as I am. What a weight off my shoulders! With an ounce of self-acceptance came a swell of compassion and understanding for other people. This was not a traditional religious experience, but it was certainly a spiritual one. Shifting this paradigm enabled the emotion of compassion to be expressed for myself and for others. It opened a spirit of love within me. That love, acceptance and humility are now part of my spiritual core. Gone are the days of questing for perfection and judging myself and others against an insurmountable standard. Here to stay is a quest to develop to my fullest potential, humility in accepting that I am imperfect, and a yearning to help people with an increasingly open heart. I've learned that spirituality comes from an intimate knowing of oneself and acknowledging the good, the bad and the ugly. Getting to a place of intimate self-knowledge was facilitated by my religious beliefs, but it was prayer and a personal relationship with God that gave my spirit a sense of peace. With profound self-knowledge and belief in a higher power one experiences a sense of purpose, a confidence to achieve that purpose, and the humility to know that everything in life, including life, is a gift from God. These gifts are to be cherished, nurtured and used to fulfill one's unique purpose in this world.

I am now able to gauge my motivations from the benchmark of my life's purpose. My purpose is to inspire people to take care of their bodies, their minds and their spirits so they can live more intentional, balanced and fulfilling lives.

One of the most expeditious ways to find your unique purpose is to think about and write down how and for what you want to be remembered when you physically leave this world. Then ask yourself if you are currently doing the things that will fulfill this aspiration? If not, what can you do differently, starting today, that will bring you closer in line with your purpose? It could be as simple as a word of encouragement to your children or a few hours of volunteer work each month. Or it could be as complex as returning to school or contemplating a career change.

Either way, remember your life is a gift from God. He wants you to make a positive difference in the lives of others. In doing so, you will be giving love and reaping joy, which translate into the real meaning of life in this sometimes crazy world in which we live.

Exercises

Five steps to help you determine your unique needs:

1. From the "outside-in," evaluate your life. Ask yourself the following questions:

a) Physical needs
- Do I have adequate food, shelter and safety?
- Am I honoring my body by:
  — Fueling it properly?
  — Exercising it?
  — Making it stronger?
  — Relieving muscle tension?

b) Intellectual needs
- Am I in the process of learning something new?
- Do I spend a proportionate amount of time absorbing messages that are benefiting me in a positive way?
- Am I challenging my intellect?
- Are my thoughts about myself and others positive?

c) Emotional needs
You may want to ask others in addition to yourself:
- When am I happiest?
- When am I most stressed or agitated?
- Am I making quiet time each day to listen to my emotions and what they are telling me?

d) Spiritual needs
- Do I know what my true purpose in life is?
- Am I acting out of love?
- Do I have hope for today, tomorrow and the next day?

2. Next, from the "inside out" determine what your needs and values are in each area as an individual. Reread each section of this chapter, if necessary, and write down what is truly important to you in each element of balance.

- Physical desires
- Intellectual desires
- Emotional desires
- Spiritual desires

3. Evaluate gaps between your current state of balance (Step 1) and your desired state of balance (Step 2). Some areas may be completely satisfied whereas others may be neglected or ignored.

4. Make a list of actions you can take in your life, starting tomorrow, to fulfill those desired needs. For example, if you want to complete your college degree, pick up the phone and call your local community college or university to inquire about enrollment requirements. If you want to attend your child's school play tomorrow night, announce tomorrow morning to your boss, secretary and anyone who may care that you will be leaving the office at 5:30 p.m. that evening so you can be there for the opening act. If you want to lose weight, cut back or eliminate sodas from your diet, starting tomorrow, or even today for that matter. If one of your desires is to re-establish or strengthen your faith, make a commitment to fit in a five-minute daily inspirational reading.

5. Institute a mechanism for evaluating your balanced reality versus your balanced ideal.

How often will you evaluate your results? I suggest a minimum of weekly, if not daily. Each of us only has 168 hours each week, and 42 to 56 of them should be for sleeping, which leaves at least 112 hours. What are we doing with those each week? Work most likely comes first. What takes up the second-largest chunk of your time? Taking care of your body? Your children? Your spouse or significant other? What about time for yourself? Doing absolutely nothing but watching the squirrels outside or listening to the birds or listening to yourself, the thoughts of your mind, the emotions of your spirit? Sacrilege, you say? Contemporary society would have you think that, but what about you? Who is better at taking care of you than you? Who else is going to do it if you don't? For that matter, who can? We all need some time to rejuvenate and revive our bodies, minds and spirits. It's not selfish, it's responsible. It's called honoring ourselves, and our world needs more of it.

Conclusion

My hope is that you begin to acknowledge the different aspects that make up your whole self so you can become more aware of where you stand in relationship to life balance. It is critical to recognize and understand the interactions between each element of our selves.

For instance, how you take care of yourself physically has an impact on your mental state, and your mental state has an impact on your feelings, and your feelings are giving you messages about your spirit. All are interrelated. It takes intentional assessment of each element to effectively determine your individual needs and begin making proactive choices to achieve a life full of balance and purpose that is distinctively and intentionally yours.

ABOUT LAURIE SANTULLI

Laurie Santulli is founder and president of Sound Decisions, a consulting firm dedicated to optimizing organizational and personal effectiveness through motivational health and productivity programs. Her thought-provoking and exciting programs create more productive and effective employees both on and off the job. This vitality translates into greater success for organizations through increased productivity, improved morale, more effective work teams and creative problem solving.

Although coming from a traditional corporate background, Laurie has experienced firsthand the benefits of the mind-body connection. She has a lifelong passion for health and brings more than 15 years of professional expertise to her clients. She holds a master's degree in Business Administration, a bachelor's in Engineering and is recognized by the International Association of Facilitators as a Certified Professional Facilitator. She also is a champion natural bodybuilder, a Certified Personal Trainer and Group Fitness Instructor. She believes it is the power of the mind that makes something seemingly impossible at first and then incredibly possible.

Laurie's background as a corporate professional with organizations including IBM, Sprint, and AT&T combined with her experience in competitive bodybuilding and professional coaching, gives her a unique perspective into the demands a challenging career can have on an executive's health. She puts this knowledge to work in her speaking programs, consulting, and educational materials, which show professionals at all levels how to, not only manage stress, but triumph over it.

Contact Information:
Laurie Santulli
Sound Decisions Consulting, Inc.
P.O. Box 270996
Tampa, FL 33688-0996
Phone: (813) 908-0000
Fax: (813) 908-1460
E-mail: LSantul@tampabay.rr.com
Website: www.sounddecisions.net

Be Organized for Balance

by Karen Ussery

You're ready for a balanced life. You want that experience of equilibrium, or *harmonious proportion,* between the areas of importance in your life. Good. Let's talk about how to organize yourself for balance.

Before you run screaming in the other direction, hear me out. Being organized does not mean you have to be like Martha Stewart or Felix Unger. In fact, many people confuse being organized with being neat. They're not the same thing. It is possible to be organized, and not be neat, and vice-versa. Being organized does not mean you have to be fanatical about your schedule, nor does it mean you have to set your life to be rigid and constricting. The first rule in organizing? There's no one right way to do it — except for the way that works for you.

Why bother getting organized? For me, the answer has always been balance. Confession time: I was not born organized. In fact, when I was a kid, my room was such a disaster zone, that my dad would tell me each night, "Karen, before you go to sleep, you need to clear a path from your bed to the door so you can get out if there's a fire."

Being organized, and living in balance, was something I learned about in my first big corporate job. I had too much to do not to be organized. I quickly discovered that the more organized I got, the easier my life was. I also learned an important lesson about balance. I worked at least twelve hours every day — sometimes even fifteen. My main food groups consisted of sugar, caffeine and Taco Bell. Not pretty. I learned about the importance of balance by being decidedly out of balance. After working that way for two years, my health and relationships were in jeopardy. I was cured of ever wanting to be out of balance again.

Hopefully, you're not living as unbalanced a life as I was. Wherever you are on the scale, the first thing to look at is why bother getting organized? What do you want to be organized for? And just what does balance mean to you anyway? It's clearly impossible to spend equal amounts of time in every area of life, so what are those areas of importance that you want to dedicate your precious time to? How could being more organized help you achieve balance?

Let's start with your life and what's important to you. Sometimes we feel out of whack without exactly knowing why. Other times it's very clear to us that one part of life is getting much more attention than another. To get organized for balance, start by listing what parts of your life you want to make time for. Tell the truth to yourself. If exercise, for example, really isn't on your list now, but you write it down because you think it *should* be, take it off. This list is for you. No guilt. Include things that are important to you that you're already spending time on. What about things you've been putting off, but that you really want to do? Write them down. You may even want to give yourself a day to really ruminate about this list. Make sure that what ends up on your life priorities list inspires you.

Once you have your guilt-free list of what's important to you, you can start with the three keys to getting organized for balance.

The first, and this is my favorite, is to simplify. I certainly would not ask you to start adding more things into your life without removing some of the dead wood first. Yet that's exactly what we tend to do when looking at how to balance. We ask ourselves, "What do I need more of? And where can I squeeze it in?" So let's start by simplifying. Before I get into the "how to" of simplifying, I want to tell you a story about my Uncle Bob. Uncle Bob was an airline pilot and would visit us on his travels. One time, we had been catching up for a while when he suddenly looked at his watch, stood up, and announced, "It's time to feed my fish." He marched over the to the telephone, dialed, waited a few moments, then hung up. He sat back down with a satisfied grin on his face, clearly amused by our puzzled looks. He explained, "I took the cover off an old rotary phone, you know, the kind with the actual bell inside. I attached a wire hanger to the hammer between the bells, bent the hanger, and taped the fish food to the other end. That way, when the phone rings, the hammer moves the hanger, and gently shakes the fish food into the water. I even timed it, so I know that three rings dispenses the appropriate amount of food."

Brilliant, right? Except he forgot one small detail: the fact that other people called! Yes, this story has a sad ending indeed. You may be aware that when you overfeed fish, they die. When he got home all the fish were belly up. What's my point? Keep it simple! Sometimes we get so caught up in setting up fancy solutions to our problems that we overlook the obvious.

Keeping that in mind, I invite you to declutter three things in your life: your stuff, your activities, and even your people.

We may feel like there's not enough time, but I never hear people complaining about not having enough stuff! (You might think you have the wrong stuff, but that's another story.) Stuff happens. Clutter happens. We live in a culture of getting.

When my husband Raymond and I were preparing to move into our second home, we were faced with the challenge of packing up the garage in our first home. Our first house was a darling, historic, tiny casita with a detached garage, as was the style in the 1940s. The garage was in the back yard, and too inconvenient for parking the cars, so what do you suppose happened over the course of the three years we lived there? You guessed it — *stuff* happened. Another feature of our historic home was minuscule closets, so anytime there wasn't a spot for something in the house, it landed in the garage. By the time we were challenged with packing it up, it was dusty and cluttered, not to mention a Holiday Inn for spiders.

And then the real problem hit me. Our "new" home was actually even older. It was built in the early 1920s, when people were just beginning to drive cars. It didn't even have a carport, never mind a free-standing garage! Although the house itself was much bigger than the first one, it had only one small utility room and a storage closet under the stairs, which narrowed down to nothing at the end.

I turned to Raymond, distraught, and asked him,. "Where are we going to put all this stuff?"

He turned to me, and in a very Zen moment asked, "Honey, why do we have to have that stuff?"

I was stunned. It was our stuff! We had to move it, didn't we? We had kept it this long, it must be good, right? After all, it was ours.

But then I realized the trouble my automatic thinking was getting me in. Who says we need that stuff? What was in there anyway? We did end up moving most of it over, but as we unpacked it, we were ruthless. If we didn't love it or use it, out it went. We had a yard sale, and whatever didn't get sold, we took to charity that day. We started life in our new house clutter-free.

Now the hidden blessing of having limited storage is that it forces us to keep the clutter down. If we don't love it or use it, it's gone. We practice the "one new thing in, one old thing out" rule every time we buy clothes. In fact, we keep a bag or two going in the guest room closet of stuff we're ready to part with. Whenever a charity calls and says it has a truck in our neighborhood, we say come on over!

Decluttering your stuff feels great. It gives you energy. If you've got a lot to go through, I recommend recruiting a buddy to help you. Or hire a professional organizer. Or use a timer and just chip away at it, 30 minutes a pop. Just let it go. I had a client who liked to say, "When in doubt, throw it out."

Next, look at the activities you can let go. What do you spend time on that's no longer meaningful for you? Maybe you made a commitment to an organization or to another person that was fun when you started, but has run its course. Or maybe you just found yourself doing extra things each week because no one else would.

What are you spending time on that you could delegate? Or asked another way, what do you spend time on that's not the best use of your time? Do you absolutely love cleaning your house or mowing your lawn? No? Have someone else do it. What about errands or office administration? You can hire people, even for just a few hours a month, to handle some of the trivia for you. One of the best delegations I ever made was having the teenage daughter of some friends do my postcard mailer. I used to send a marketing postcard to 800 clients each month. That meant 800 labels and 800 stamps. Took me four hours. I asked Melissa to do it for $40 and she was delighted. Better yet, I was delighted!

I had also been considering hiring someone for yard maintenance but I'd heard it was expensive. One day, I broke down and asked a guy who was doing my neighbor's yard to look at mine and give me a quote. It was about a quarter of the price I expected! Needless to say, he was hired on the spot. Sometimes, you just can't afford not to. People love to help. Ask your kids, your neighbors, the stay-at-home mom down the street.

Now, decluttering people. This may be a tough one: Who is a vampire in your life? Who is sucking your energy and enthusiasm every time you see them or talk to them? Although it's hard, sometimes it's time to let certain people go, even if they're related. If you can't transform the relationship, it may be time to end it. It doesn't serve you or them to stay in it, quietly resentful.

I encourage you to make a list of ten items, activities or people you are ready to declutter from your life. Or, just put this book down and go do it right now.

Now that you've simplified, you've got some room for important things. You have more energy from decluttering stuff and people, and you've got more time from decluttering your calendar. The next key in organizing your life for balance is to schedule your priorities.

Here's the bottom line: if it's truly important to you, it needs to be on your schedule. Otherwise, you're leaving the most vital things in your life up to chance. You may have heard the story of the old executive on his deathbed, lamenting, of course, not missed opportunities at work, but at home. He had a simple wish: that he'd spent more time with his family than at the office. I'm sure many of us can relate.

So what's truly important to you? Start with the list you already made. If you still need to work on it, consider these arenas: family, relationships, home, leisure, hobby, sports, work, financial, health, spiritual, educational, community, social. Again, I am not saying you *should* have goals and objectives in each of these areas. Rather, consider this list as a springboard from which to determine what you want on your list right now.

My husband works into the evening, so we schedule our mornings together. I mean, we have it worked out to the minute! We make time for prayer and meditation, we go for a run together, I make breakfast while he showers, we eat together, he leaves, and I go get ready. It works! It's a good time for us to connect with each other and have a great start to the day. We fine-tune as needed. If we did not have it scheduled, there is no way we'd have that productive time together each day. I'd just keep hitting that snooze alarm. Honestly, although I love to exercise, it's rare when I *feel* like going for a jog, especially when it's cold and dark out. If you want it to happen, schedule it.

Here's a powerful habit: Once a week, take your life priority list out, open up your calendar, and start scheduling. Some of the items on your list may be daily, like exercise, some may be weekly, like date night with your sweetheart, and some of them may be long-term, such as specific actions you need to take to get you to a bigger goal. For example, if you're planning on taking a two-week vacation in six months, what action do you need to take this week? Get on the internet? Call your travel agent? Get the actions scheduled. If you make this a weekly practice, you'll be amazed at what you achieve.

What about scheduling individual time with each person in your family? Kids love it when they get Dad or Mom all to themselves and don't have to share with siblings. Just as important, what about time for you? When I start getting cranky about how busy I am, Raymond gently asks me, "Honey, do you have any Karen time scheduled in?" Karen time for me is time that is scheduled, but unstructured. It is not time to get caught up on chores. It is mine to do with whatever I feel in that moment. It's not a luxury, it's a necessity.

For most of us, it's easier to honor the appointments we have with others than the ones we make with ourselves. I say it's just as critical to honor the latter. Just as you would for an important client, be on time, be prepared, and be dressed appropriately for your down time.

One of my girlfriends and I get together every two weeks (and of course we schedule the next meeting each time we meet, otherwise we will never find the time). I asked her once how meeting every other week worked for her, as she had three children under the age of six at home, she worked full-time as a scientist, plus she did volunteer work. Her answer was very wise. She said "First of all, my kids come first. But this time with my friends rejuvenates me. And if I'm not taking care of me, I'm no good with them. Just as important, I want my girls to grow up knowing that it's OK for them to take care of themselves first."

There's a distinction between being selfish and being self-interested. Being selfish is having no concern for how your actions affect another. Being self-interested is making sure you are getting your needs met. You are the one responsible for you, and the only one who can make sure your life works. Make sure your schedule reflects that. OK, now your life is simplified. You are regularly scheduling in that which is important. How do you maintain this balance? The third key is to say "no." No is a wonderful tool. Use it often.

At the risk of offending my sisters, I will say this: there is one particular gender who is generally not as good at saying no as another particular gender. It's what we were brought up to believe. It's not nice to say no. Well, I'm here to say it's just fine! It's everyone's right. And some of us are really going to have to practice this one.

My husband Raymond has always been better at saying no than I have been. But I'm getting better! When we were in college, we were typical ramen noodle-eating students, and going out for a meal was a real treat. One weekend my mother came for a visit. She and I were up early talking, when she offered to take us out for breakfast. Excellent! I rushed to wake Raymond up for this wonderful opportunity. Free breakfast out at a nice restaurant. It doesn't get much better when you're a starving college student.

I went to the bed where he was sleeping soundly, gently touched his face, and said quietly, "Raymond, Mom wants to take us to breakfast."

I thought he would be as delighted with this news as was I, but he rolled over without opening his eyes, and said, "I'm kind of busy right now."

As I said, he's good at saying no!

As a professional organizer, here's a reality I see every day: there is more to do, more to know, and more stuff to have than we could possibly do, know or have. There is so much coming at us each day, we absolutely must prioritize. Advertisers know this. They do everything to get our scattered attention. Sometimes we get sucked into believing that, just because it's good information, I must know it. Or, this is perfectly useful, therefore I should keep it. We spend so much time trying to do or know everything, it's impossible to go deep with anything. We are simply spread too thin.

There is power in saying no.

OK, so maybe at this point you fully agree with me, but you're still not comfortable actually saying the word no. Well, I have some tips for you on how to make no a little less painful.

First, a simple substitute for no. "Sorry, I have other plans." The other person doesn't need to know that your other plans are to be sitting on your couch, watching a movie.

Or try this: when someone invites you to do something, postpone your decision. Say, "Hmm, I'm going to have to check my schedule and get back to you on this." That will give you some time to see if it's really something you want to do, and if it really fits into your calendar, and if it is either on, or consistent with, your life priority list. Even better, when appropriate, is to ask *them* to get back with *you*. By putting the ball back in their court, sometimes they'll just lob it to someone else.

By the way, if you have someone in your life who doesn't accept your saying no, please refer to the first key of balancing your life — decluttering people. Someone who won't respect your boundaries is a good one for that list.

Living in balance is possible. It's learned, not genetic. Use the three keys. Simplify to make room and declutter the accumulation. Schedule that which is truly important. And say no as needed, to keep it all in balance.

ABOUT KAREN USSERY

Karen Ussery has been making her living from other people's disorders since 1995. A Professional Organizer and Speaker, she's the owner of Organized for Success. She leads seminars and consults business people in organization, productivity and life balance.

A member of the National Association of Professional Organizers, Karen is also the Founder of the Arizona Professional Organizers Association. She has written numerous articles on organizing the office and was the technical editor for the Complete Idiot's Guide to Organizing Your Life. *She is the author of an idea-a-week book called* Organized for Success: 52 Organizing and Time Management Solutions for Busy Professionals.

Contact Information:
Karen Ussery
Organized for Success
56 West Windsor Ave.
Phoenix, AZ 85003
Phone: (602) 248-2884
Fax; (602) 266-2101
Website: www.organizedforsuccess.com

WHO TEETERED YOUR TOTTER?

by Ann Wright

Inner Peace is knowing that you have balance in your life and are investing time in a variety of areas. No one thing should ever be your whole life. For if it were taken away where would you be?

Remember those carefree days as a kid? You know, the days you went to the park and found time to play on every single piece of equipment you could find. Oh, to again be able to touch those pearly white clouds from the swing, feel the ever so sweet breeze on your face as you speed quickly down the slide and swing from ring to ring on the monkey bars, hoping no one would see the effort and pain it took to really get yourself from one to the other. And then there was that silly teeter-totter. You know, the seesaw that you and your friend were always trying to balance. However, because of a difference in weight, it continually went up and down unless you adjusted where each of you sat. Of course, there was always one "friend" that jumped off and let you fall quickly to the ground. Ohhhh, did that ever hurt! Ever feel that life has gotten out of control and has let you fall to the cold, hard ground just like that "friend" on the other end of the teeter-totter? I believe there are days many of us feel as if life is completely out of balance, just like it was when we were on that teeter-totter years ago.

What does it take to achieve balance in your life? I believe it takes hard work, plus strong desire, commitment, and constant attention to priorities to achieve balance in life. I also think it takes a plan. Whether or not it's our entire life or only a portion of our life that's "out of balance," many of us ask ourselves, "How did life get so far out of whack?" I have asked myself that question many times over. Who did teeter my totter and how do I get back in sync? Whether working to achieve balance at home, work, or both, I have developed and utilized a simple, yet successful, practical, common sense approach to achieving balance in my life. Whether working to achieve balance in life in general or for a specific area of your life (for example, your career) this process works. When working to commit a process to memory, the use of an acronym that is topic related makes the task easier. Hence, the acronym for my process is — you guessed it — BALANCE.

If you feel, like many of us, that your life is out of balance, you have probably 1) said to yourself "someone has teetered my totter and my life is out of balance," 2) made the conscious decision to change things to get balance back into your life, and 3) committed to working through a process to achieve balance in your life. So now it's time to get down to business.

First, since you are serious about achieving balance in your life, set aside some quiet time to actually work through the process. Find a place where you feel comfortable and can at least hear yourself think while you work on this potentially life-changing plan to achieve balance that will ultimately result in peace of mind. Committing your plan to paper will help make it real. Michele Matt (a good friend and author) once told me, if you "think it, ink it." In an effort to assist you with this process, there is an outline you can use at the end of this chapter. Feel free to write in the book or make copies and enlarge them for your own personal use. (Little did you know this was going to be a "working chapter.") Remember, you can be as broad or specific as you want when working through this process. For instance, you can use it for looking at your whole life to using it for a specific project when working with a team.

Let's get started.

Begin with a vision.

Close your eyes and ask yourself: if I were painting a picture of my life (or day, depending on which aspect of your life you're working) how would I want it to look? Where and how would I/should I be spending my time? Toward what outcome am I working? If you don't know where you're going, there's a good chance you'll never get there.

I am reminded of a story, from the well-known book *Alice in Wonderland and Through the Looking-Glass* by Lewis Carroll, about my favorite animal — the cat.

The Wise Cheshire Cat and Alice

One day Alice was running all around Wonderland when she came to a fork in the road. In a quandary she said to herself or so she thought, "Which way do I go? Which way do I go?" Little did she know that the wise Cheshire cat was gazing down at her. He yawned and very slowly asked Alice "Where are you going?" Alice innocently replied, "I don't know." With a smile and a sneer, the Cheshire cat stated, in a very matter of fact tone of voice, "Then it doesn't much matter which road you take, if you don't know where you're going."

There's much to be said for the encounter between Alice and the Cheshire cat. Is the picture you have in your mind clear and concise? Can you see yourself living that balanced life you're dreaming of?

Assess where you are.

Ever wonder at the end of the day where in the world did the time go? What did I accomplish? It is in this phase that you take an inventory of how you are actually spending your time. Be honest with yourself. Use the form at the end of this chapter as a guide to keep track of where and how long you spend your time on any given item.

Whether you're taking inventory of your life as a whole or one specific area such as a workday will determine the type of inventory you take and list you develop. Remember to be very specific about what you're doing and for how long. For example, if you watch TV three or four hours a day, write it down. There are no right or wrong answers, nor is there anyone watching over your shoulder saying, "Oh, so that's where all his/her time goes." The more honest you are in this phase of the process, the more successful you will be in the following phases.

For example you may ask yourself:

- How much time am I on the phone?
- Do I jump from one project to the next before completing anything of substance?
- Am I constantly interrupted by others or perhaps even by myself? I know you're thinking, "How do I interrupt myself?" I used to do it all the time. You know, make a couple of phone calls, check e-mail several times a day (or minute), start and stop various projects and never finish one of them.
- Am I working on my A priorities or my C priorities because the latter can be done quickly and without much thought? Besides, the more items I check off my list, the more productive I've been, right? Wrong.

Maybe the reason your life is spiraling out of control and you feel as if you've lost control and life isn't in balance is that you're spending time on the things that aren't really that important; you only think they are.

Listen to your heart and list your priorities

Ever have one of those really tough decisions to make. You know, the kind that keeps you up at night? I remember in December of 1993 having to make an extremely tough decision. Maybe to some of you it won't seem like a tough decision on the surface; however, it was a decision that would affect the path my life would take and affect where I am today. Working full time and being involved full time in the Iowa Jaycees took most of my waking hours and then some. I had worked my way up in the Jaycee organization and was in a position to run for president of the Iowa Jaycees, a goal that had been mine for more years than I could count. Opportunities had presented themselves along the way, and I had been lucky and wise enough to take advantage of them. December was the deciding month. Was I going to move on and run for state president, and, if successful, be in a position to become national vice president the following year and then the first woman national president? The thought of it made my head spin and heart race.

Thinking that life was out of control caused me to have doubts about what I thought was my ultimate goal. In order to decide whether or not I was going to follow my dream, I went to, where else, the mall. With an extra large diet Pepsi, a thick pad of paper and pen in hand, I sat down in the midst of busy shoppers and began to list my priorities, one by one. Beginning with writing down how I pictured my life and where I saw myself in ten years, five years, one year and tomorrow and then what it would take to get me there, I listed my priorities, not only the ones that were in my head, but those in my heart. Seeing things in black and white made a big difference.

In my mind I painted a picture of how I wanted my life to look. I saw myself:

- Investing time in a new relationship
- Finishing my education by earning my Bachelor's degree
- Starting my own business
- Becoming an accomplished speaker, trainer and writer
- Having a family

Can you guess what my decision was? I didn't run for president of the Iowa Jaycees. I invested time in that new relationship, married Doug five years later, finished my degree, started a family, have my own business and am working on becoming that accomplished speaker, trainer and writer.

What does your heart tell you your priorities are?

Analyze and take action.

Based on your work to date (and you thought you were just going to be reading this chapter; little did you know you would have the opportunity to work) you now know:

- What you want your life to look like
- Where you're spending your time
- What your priorities are

In this step of the process you have to take a long, hard look at how and where you are spending your time. Analyze every area of your life or day, depending on what area you are working.

Ask yourself, what is it going to take for me to get my life in balance with regard to what's important to me? Is where I'm spending my time helping me achieve true balance in my life? If yes, great, keep doing what you're doing; if your answer is no, what action do you need to take to get your life in balance?

Questions you may want to ask yourself:

- Am I spending an extraordinary amount of time at work when I really want to spend more time with my family?
- Am I spending too much time in front of the TV when I really need to be spending some extra time working on my career or volunteering?
- Am I spending too much time with my friends when what I really want is some time to myself?
- Am I spending too much time on the phone or maybe the Internet wandering aimlessly in cyberspace without an outcome in mind when I could be reading a book, fishing or scrapbooking?

If you are challenged with everyday balance at work, ask yourself some of the following questions:

- Am I spending too much time on idle chatter?
- Am I spending enough time with those that I supervise or with my peers?
- Am I spending too much time on those C priorities because the A ones are going to take quite a bit of thought and work?
- Am I working on my most challenging projects when I'm at my peak or when I am tired?
- Do I say yes to everything because I want everyone to think I'm superman or superwoman when I need to learn to say no?

• Do I set realistic deadlines?

The answers to some of these questions may not only surprise you but help you to find out why you spend time on the things you do, instead of on the things you either should be spending time on or want to spend time on.

Negotiate with whom you need.

To get where you want to be, it may mean negotiating with your supervisor, your significant other, your children or even yourself!

Negotiation: it sounds so simple, yet for many can be so difficult. Maybe it's the fear of not getting what you want or appearing to be selfish that keeps us from negotiating with those who can help us. When you negotiate with someone, each party should get something of value. I am a firm believer in Steven Covey and his concept of win-win. Each of us values different things and has different priorities at various times in our lives. Communication is the key. My mom used to tell me God gave us two ears and one mouth for a reason. Listen to what people are saying; this includes yourself.

Ask yourself, "With whom do I need to negotiate to achieve the balance I so desire?" Perhaps the first person you need to negotiate with is yourself. Many people never think about negotiating with themselves. What are you willing to sacrifice in order to achieve what you truly want? Oprah Winfrey said it so well, "You can have it all, just not at the same time."

Negotiating with others is sometimes more challenging because they, too, are working to achieve balance in their lives and juggling all of life's priorities. What can you expect others to give up to help you? What are you willing to do to help them achieve balance in their lives? In order to achieve balance in my life, Doug, my husband, and I changed our lifestyle so I could stay at home when our son was little. We negotiated the type of lifestyle we would have and what each was and was not willing to give up to have balance between raising Noah and still working to achieve our personal and professional goals. In balancing home, work and school, Doug works during the day and attends school two nights a week while I stay at home with Noah during the day, teach at night, facilitate workshops and speak on a limited basis until Noah goes to school. Both of us are in charge of household chores, take time for ourselves and even make time for a date with each other now and then. Though family comes first, when it came time to writing this chapter, I negotiated with Doug and Noah for time to write. We agreed Doug would play with Noah so I could write and I would play with Noah the next day so he could finish his research paper. Noah wanted to play Clifford on the computer; however, since I needed the computer, he negotiated himself a fishing expedition with his Dad.

Sometimes you have to negotiate with a supervisor or peer. This can be difficult, yet very rewarding. The majority of people are working to balance their time so they can achieve their goals at work, be successful and still have free time. Ask your peers or your team what their priorities are and how you can help them reach their goals. When people know you are concerned with helping them, they will be more interested in helping you. With a supervisor, priorities may have to be discussed, theirs and yours. If, in fact, there is physically not enough time to complete all assigned tasks, you may have to renegotiate deadlines and/or work assignments. Be part of the solution, not the problem. Go in with a plan.

Are you ready for the next step; you know, that six-letter word that everyone loves to hate, but is a necessity in life?

Change

Commit to making the changes necessary to achieve your goals and create balance in your life.

"If you always do what you've always done,
you'll always get what you've always gotten."
— Author unknown

It's true. If you keep doing what you're doing and you're not getting the balance you desire, you have to commit to changing whatever it is you're doing. Change is that six-letter word which can help you achieve the balance for which you've been looking. How many people do you know that talk and talk and talk about changing, but never do? It usually takes 21 days to change a habit and incorporate it into your lifestyle. In the big scheme of things, 21 days isn't that long. Just remember: short-term pain for long-term gain.

Commitment is a big part of the change. You have to commit to changing what you're doing. Following are a couple of simple examples of how you might change what you're doing to what you should be doing to achieve balance.

- Maybe you've decided that you watch too much TV when you could be spending time reading, playing with your children, or exercising. What are you going to change? Turn off the TV for good? That's a bit drastic don't you think? What about limiting yourself to a certain amount of TV. You haven't given it up completely; you'll just have to be more selective with what you watch. You could find yourself with 5-10 extra hours a week.
- So you want to exercise more? Change your early morning habits. Commit to getting up one hour earlier three mornings a week. I did and it's working great. I've been walking three times a week for over a year.
- What about spending more time with your employees if you're a supervisor? Commit to meeting with them face-to-face or via phone once a week or whatever is necessary.

Changing isn't easy, nor is it that difficult. Make the decision to change, decide what to change, stick to it and just do it.

"Remember this; when you're through changing . . . You're through."
— Author unknown

Evaluate and Enjoy

After making those important changes, ask yourself how is it working? Celebrate what the changes have brought to your life — hopefully, the balance for which you've been looking.

Evaluation. In business, evaluation is used all the time, but how many of us, after working so hard on changing things, ever take the time to evaluate whether or not the changes have helped us get where we want to be? It's imperative that we take the time to look at the changes we have made and whether or not they have helped us. If the changes are working, great; keep doing what you are doing. If they aren't, work through the process again and determine what other changes need to be made. It'll be a lot easier the second time around. No matter what the outcome, pat yourself on the back and celebrate the fact that you had the courage to sit down, take a long hard look at your life or project and change what needed changing. Change is hard. Many people talk about change and how they wish things were but never make the effort to change things because it's just too hard. They accept the status quo. So if the changes you have made have helped get your life into balance, celebrate. Enjoy your newfound balance. You might even share with someone how you achieved balance in your life and help him or her achieve balance.

It is my sincere hope that this process will assist you in finding that all-important balance in your life, which usually leads to inner peace. Life may continue to feel like a teeter-totter and you may still ask yourself "Who teetered my totter?" However, the bottom line is that no matter who teetered your totter you are the only one that can put your life back into balance. It may depend on making hard choices, but the end result will truly be worth it. Good luck!

Your Balance Sheets

Begin with a vision. (What do you want your life to look like? This can be used for your whole life, a day or a project.)

If I could picture my life/day/project perfectly balanced it would look like the following (be specific):

____

____

____

____

____

Assess where you are and inventory your time.

I am spending my time doing the following:

Activity	**Time spent on it**
______________________________	__________
______________________________	__________
______________________________	__________
______________________________	__________
______________________________	__________

Listen to your heart and list your priorities.

The priorities in my life are: (Just start listing your priorities and where you want to spend your time. You can always go back and put them in order of priority. You may find you have to make choices as to what your priorities are now and re-prioritize in the future.)

____

____

____

____

____

Analyze and take action.

Based upon what my priorities are and where I'm spending my time, where is my time being spent that it either shouldn't be or should be reduced?

____

____

____

____

____

Negotiate with whom you need to.

I need to negotiate the following tasks with whom?

Item which needs to be negotiated	**Person with whom I need to negotiate**
________________	________________
________________	________________
________________	________________
________________	________________
________________	________________

Change

I commit to making the following changes.

Change to be made	**Date by when the change will be made**
________________	________________
________________	________________
________________	________________
________________	________________
________________	________________

Evaluate and Enjoy

The change made	**Is it working for me?** If yes, great; if no, what will I change?
______________________________	______________________________
______________________________	______________________________
______________________________	______________________________
______________________________	______________________________
______________________________	______________________________
______________________________	______________________________

ABOUT ANN WRIGHT

Ann Wright, owner of The Wright Solutions, works with people on developing their life skills so they can aspire to their career and personal goals. As a learning and development professional she has worked with many diverse participants across the United State and understands the way people learn to maximize individual performance. Known for her high-energy presentation skills, Ann can delight and entertain her audience as well as educate and get results. Workshop topics Ann facilitates include: Attitude, Time Management, Goal Setting, Teambuilding, Customer Service, Stress Management and Working Effectively with Volunteers. Ann works with her clients to customize the workshops in order to best meet the needs of the client. With over twenty years experience in the areas of leadership, management and training she believes that people are an organization's most valuable asset.

Ann is an active member of ASTD (American Society for Trainers & Developers) and an affiliate of the National Speakers Association, Iowa Chapter. She is a life long member of the United States Junior Chamber of Commerce and was named one of the ten outstanding Iowans by the Iowa Junior Chamber of Commerce in 1997. She is also a contributing author to the book, Rekindling the Human Spirit.

Contact Information:
Ann Wright
The Wright Solutions
4321 Wakonda Drive
Norwalk IA 50211
Phone: (515) 285-8154
E-mail: Wrightsolutions@juno.com

What Do You Want? The Not-so-Simple Question

by David Mee-Lee, M.D.

When I was in medical school, they taught me to first ask the patient, "What is the presenting complaint?" Or in other words, "What do you want?" Of course, we weren't supposed to just fire that question at the patient. We were supposed to have some bedside manner and say something like "How can I help you today?" Or, "What brought you here today?" Then we were to listen to the patient and hear what he had to say. But actually, a study reported in the *Journal of the American Medical Association* found that doctors typically will listen to a patient's opening statement for little more than 23 seconds before changing the subject or "redirecting" the talk. That doesn't give you much time to say what you want — if you even know what you want.

But here, you will have all the time you want for this not-so-simple question. Take your time and explore with me. At the end of the process of answering this question for yourself, however, you should be able to really zero in and say what you want in 23 seconds or less. Why is that skill important and useful? Because knowing what you want — really want — can focus your energies, unleash your creativity, decrease your stress and enrich not only your life, but also those around you. Most of the time, we think we know what we want in our relationships, work, social life and where and how we live. But in the busy-ness of life, we're often just reacting, not choosing our reactions; just existing, not creating the life and love we want.

Driving Myself Crazy

Here's a recent example of how I created my own stress and wasted energy rather than creating peace and serenity — all in a simple visit to the post office. Due to budget cutbacks, some postal branches in my town have closed, resulting in long lines and waiting times at the main facility. Here are seven ways I drove myself crazy that day in the post office:

1. I arrived and saw the long line snaking out into the lobby and immediately huffed and puffed and rolled my eyes with frustration.

2. I noticed a postal employee in the back behind the desk clerks. I started getting annoyed that he was not helping reduce wait times. Logically, I knew he may have a different job, but that didn't stop me judging him for not helping.

3. When another clerk arrived, she took forever to log in and start serving customers. "What does it take to put her stamps and money in the drawer and punch her password into the computer?" I fumed to myself.

4. A clerk became available, but the next person in line was not watching. The line slowed as people waved, called out, and signaled him to proceed to the next open counter. Again I fumed inside: "Why can't people be watching? Don't they know the line is long? How can you be so out of it not to be ready to proceed as soon as a clerk opens up?"

5. Another clerk became available. This time, the next in line did notice, but sauntered ever so slowly to the booth. I wasted energy analyzing and judging this person: "Is this some kind of passive aggressive act — walking so slowly when everyone wants the line to move along?"

6. With two people served in quick succession, now the line was moving nicely. But could you believe it? The next two in line were talking and socializing, and didn't immediately take up

the slack and advance. Another chance to fume inside: "Will you two please watch — can't you see we want the line to move. Take up the slack and quit talking so much!"

7. Now it is finally my turn and I buy my stamps. Then the postal worker starts his litany of services: Do I want to insure the letter? How about Priority Mail? Return Receipt Request by any chance? How about other stamps? This was getting worse than a telemarketer interrupting my dinner. "Just give me the stamps and let me get out of here." I smiled all through this, only adding to my stress, as my face didn't match what I was thinking or feeling inside.

Before you judge me too much, look inside your memory banks and see if you can identify. If not in the post office, check how you drive on the road, or how you behave in the checkout line of the supermarket, or how you treated your loved ones recently. *If you cannot relate in any way, congratulations!* Celebrate whatever self-care methods keep you in balance in work, love and play. For me, it made me think twice. Do I really want to live like this? Judging people I don't even know, fuming inside about people and situations over which I have no control, faking nice when I am really stressed and impatient?

The more clear you are on what you want, the quicker you are at choosing how you live and create the peace and balance that keeps you cool, calmed and collected. Instead of figuring out 23 hours later all the little reactive stress points that sapped your energy and made it a stressful day, you can intervene to cut the reactions dead in their tracks — maybe even in 23 seconds instead.

Double, Triple Meanings and More

Before we start exploring the question, "What do you want?" some more observations suggest why this is not a simple inquiry. Think of all the different meanings that this apparently straightforward query can represent.

- "WHAT DO YOU WANT?" — shouted the teen to her mother, meaning, "Leave me alone."
- "What do you WANT?" — said the frustrated mother curtly in the candy store where her son repeatedly changed his mind on which candy to have — "We don't have all day. Pick one, choose anything, but let's go."
- "What do YOU want?" — sighed the tired teacher irritably after a long line of requests for extra time on the homework project — "I'm tired and want to go; can't it wait?"
- "*What do you want?*" — said the scantily clad, exotic entertainer coquettishly in the gentleman's club, meaning, "I'm available . . . for a fee."
- "What DO you want?" — she said impatiently as she confronted her commitment phobic, six-year-long boyfriend who delayed once again their formal engagement announcement. What she means is: "Marry me or I'm out of here."

So as you focus on achieving balance, you can either drive yourself crazy, or you can be in the driver's seat of your own life. But balance starts with knowing what you want. And because there are multiple meanings to that question, let's help you become your own shrink for a few moments. You may even save yourself those $200 visits to the psychiatrist. Take your time to explore each part of this important question.

You choose what the *focus* of your exploration is about. Do you want to know what you want in your career? Remember, if you find a job you love, you'll never work another day in your life (or that's what the billboard for a vocational counseling center said). Do you want to know what a balanced life for you means? Do you want to exercise more? Eat more healthily? Communicate more compassionately? Play more spontaneously? Or is the focus on what you want in your love life? What kind of relationship? What kind of communication? What kind of intimacy?

It is best to focus on each part of the question before moving onto the next part — that 23-second, focused summary of what you really want awaits you at the end.

WHAT Do You Want?
Brainstorming All the Possibilities and Options

Once you have chosen the focus of exploration (and you can repeat this process for different arenas of life), let your mind go into brainstorming mode and list *all* the possibilities — however broad and bizarre they may be. The **WHAT** part of the exploration phase is keeping all your options open. This gives you the broadest possible selection from which to start the focusing process.

Focus: ________________________ (*e.g., my work, my daily life, my health, my communication, my play life, my love life, or my relationships*)

WHAT is my brainstorming list of all possibilities? (*e.g., work less, commute less, have more autonomy; have more time to myself, less stress, more balance; exercise more, meditate more, eat better food; yell less, be more loving, have more fun*):

____________________ ____________________

____________________ ____________________

____________________ ____________________

____________________ ____________________

____________________ ____________________

____________________ ____________________

When you are comfortable with your exhaustive list of possibilities, the next step is to begin to pare that broad list down to a narrower choice of priorities. (Use additional pages if you need more space for your **WHAT** list). Which of these do you really want to focus on? Of all the options, which ones are the dominant options (**DO**)? Which do you feel are definite options (**DO**)? Which options would you definitely want on the to do list?

What DO You Want?
What are the Dominant Options and Definite Options?

Pros and Cons: Benefits and Costs

Stay Employed at this Job		Leave and Start my Own Business	
Pros/Benefits	**Cons/Costs**	**Pros/Benefits**	**Cons/Costs**
1. Health insurance 2. Vacation and sick pay 3. Biweekly electronic deposit to my bank 4. Like my colleagues	1. Limited advancement opportunities 2. Bored, not challenged 3. Downsizing risk 4. Don't like my boss 5. Commute is long	1. Challenging and creative 2. Can work from home 3. Autonomy 4. No long staff meetings and hassles	1. No benefits 2. Capital investment problems 3. Can I make it?

It is easy to get overwhelmed by all the possibilities. The more creative, competent and energetic a person you are, the more options there are open to you. But having too many options can paralyze you as you face the dilemma of "decisions, decisions, decisions."

So this next step of the process is important — to search yourself more deeply inside and check your heart and soul for what **DO** you really, really want? Would you care much if you did get this option or wouldn't it matter? How upset would you be if you did not do this particular choice? Is this option very important to you or someone else you care about? You could rate each possibility on a scale of 1-10 with 10 being most important to you. Then add all the options that scored 8-10 on your dominant, definite, deep and decisive options list (**DO**). Or if you are having trouble narrowing the list down, do a pros and cons, cost/benefit list for each option. (See example above.)

It's not time yet to finalize your decision. There are more discoveries and explorations to go that will help get to the heart of the matter.

Re-focus on the topic of exploration**:** For example, my work, my daily life, my health, my communication, my play life, my love life, or my relationships.

Review your **WHAT** list of all possibilities

What **DO** I want on the short list? Which are the Dominant, Definite, Deep and Decisive Options that I really want? (*Which of the options do I really care about most? How upset would I be if this option were not on the final list? Is this option a 9 or 10 in importance to me?)*:

Now that you have your short list, the next step is to focus on *who* is actually going to decide on the final list of what you want. You may say: "Me, of course, dummy. Who else?" Well let's see. This step will require you to dig more deeply into who the "me" decision maker really is — who you are — not who you think you should be; not who you think someone else wants you to be; or not what society or tradition told you to be.

What Do YOU Want?
Will the Real Decision Maker Stand Up?

If you are the oldest in your family, you may feel you have to be the responsible one. Or if your mother had an alcohol problem and you learned to survive by taking over for her, caring for your younger siblings, and putting aside your own needs and rescuing others, it is hard to stop being a people pleaser and a rescuer. Or if you came from a very highly achieving family who drove you hard to get straight A's, you may have lingering resentments that color what you choose. You may have been labeled the smart or dumb one of the family, or the black sheep, or the spirited one, or the quiet one, or the stubborn one, or daddy's right hand man, or mother's little helper or the good little boy or girl. No one was trying to squeeze you into a labeled identity box, but it happens. And now that you are older and get to choose who you are and want to be, it's not so easy to know who you are and what you want.

Maybe you were taller or shorter than your peers, or obese or all skin and bones, or your breasts were way too big or way too small. And now the you that lives life in your head is still the beanpole giraffe or the short man syndrome, or fat or skinny, or thinking that men are always looking at your chest or not looking at your chest enough. The point is that now you have become your anatomy, not your ability; your embarrassing body, not your essential beauty.

Society and the culture we live in play a big part in defining who we are. Ought-ism, not autism, is rampant. I "oughta" be the bread-winner because I'm a male. I "oughta" be the homemaker because I'm the female. I "oughta" not cry because I am a guy. I "oughta" not yell because I am a gal — it's not ladylike. I "oughta" know my place because I am a minority. There are all kinds of "isms"and prejudices that rob you of who you are when you live life *reacting* to the label instead of *choosing* who you want to be. To name a few, there are racism, sexism, ageism, and attractiveism (I made that up to mean the phenomenon where the attractive people get preferential treatment). There's nothing wrong with being a breadwinner or homemaker or sharing your emotions or not. But is this what you *chose* to be and do? Or did you fall into "ought-ism"?

Re-focus on the topic of exploration. You have your **WHAT** list of all possibilities that you narrowed to your short to **DO** list of Dominant, Definite, Deep and Decisive Options. To get to what you really want depends also on knowing who you are and who is really making the decision.

List the labels you have been living that arose from your family life *(e.g., Mr. or Ms. Responsible; rescuer or people pleaser; smart, dumb, black sheep, spirited, quiet, etc.)*

____

____

List the labels you have been living that arose from your anatomy and body type *(e.g., beanpole, short man syndrome, fatso, skinny, etc.)*

____

____

List the labels you have been living that arose from "ought-ism" or society and culture *(e.g breadwinner, homemaker, heterosexual, homosexual, the Jew, Chink, etc.)*

____

____

You get to decide and choose *who* the decision maker will be. Will it be one or more of the labels you live? Or can you see beyond the labels and know whom **YOU** choose to be? You can't divorce yourself from your history — that is part of you. But you can rise above your history and labels. You decide what combination of experiences really defines you, the decision-maker in your own life.

So now you have your short **DO** list of Dominant, Definite, Deep and Decisive Options; and you now know better *who* will be making the final choice(s) in what you want. The final step in the process is to focus like a laser on what you really want. What are the final one or two most important options from the short list that you most desire?

What Do You WANT?
Final Answer on What is Desired Most

What do you want and desire most for your work, your health, your relationships, your love life, your play life, your communication or whatever the arena of life? It may seem selfish to be so self-absorbed in what you want. Shouldn't I be deciding what is best for the company, or the team, or my spouse or partner, or the kids or society…? There's nothing wrong with thinking of others and making choices that take their feelings and needs into account. The problem is when your decisions are reactive, not proactive, are based on "ought" not thought, and based on taking care of others to the exclusion of you.

When you are clear that what you want is really what you want, you will be much closer to not driving yourself crazy. You'll need just 23 seconds to check to see if you are living "in choice," or just living and reacting. We lose our balance; get off center; increase our stress; argue and fight; sap our energy and creativity, and get unsteady, uncertain and unfocused when we have not taken the time to really choose what we want.

Re-focus on the topic of exploration. Review your short **DO** list of Dominant, Definite, Deep and Decisive Options. Reaffirm the **YOU** who will be the decision-maker.

What is the final answer on what I want? On what do I most desire to focus my energy, creativity, and singleness of purpose? (W*hich of the short list am I choosing as most important to me, not someone else? Which option speaks most to my heart, my essence, my integrity, my soul?)* Write the one or two most important choices here.

#1 ____

#2 ____

Making it Work for You

Here is an example that is not a life-changing experience, but it illustrates the value of taking the time first to choose what you really want. Have you ever shopped for a birthday gift for someone who has it all? You have no idea what the person wants or what you want to give, so you wander aimlessly through store after store hoping for inspiration. You don't want to look cheap, but you could never afford something that would impress this wealthy friend. You want to make a good impression, but you are not sure that you are all that impressive yourself. Am I trying to pretend I am in the same socioeconomic ballpark? Am I trying too hard to be liked or accepted in his circle? What do I have to give to him anyway, personally, professionally or socially?

So you stress and waste time and energy and walk out of the store frustrated, still without a gift. Then you remember that not-so-simple question: *What Do You Want?*

- ***WHAT*** do you want? — Brainstorm all the possibilities: I want to be his friend, in his social circle, considered fun to be with, exposed to his wisdom and business savvy, and viewed as competent and talented.
- What ***DO*** you want? — Which are the Dominant Options and Definite Options: I want to be seen as competent and to have the opportunity to learn from his business acumen.
- What do ***YOU*** want? — Who is the Real Decision Maker? You dig deeply. Having come from a lower socioeconomic group, you observe that you get intimidated around wealthy people. You also notice that you are self-conscious about your weak business and financial skills and sometimes feel you have no competence in anything. You know that, in fact, you are a competent musician with the guitar and an amateur songwriter and that your friend has admired your musicality in the past.
- What do you ***WANT***? — Final Answer: The most desirable gift becomes clear. You write a simple, but catchy birthday song; double-track the vocals and instruments on your computer with software that produces almost studio quality sound; burn a compact disc; and design a tasteful CD label on your home computer. The CD along with an offer to teach him the song on his expensive, but unused, guitar is a gift he absolutely loves and so do you.

The old way would have left you frustrated and stressed with a huge credit card bill for a gift you could not afford. By taking a moment to think through what you really wanted, you gave a gift that demonstrated your competence and creativity. Because you did not reactively rush into an expensive and "impressive" gift, you chose a gift that met the goals of what you wanted. You can trade your musical talents for his business knowledge and enrich each other's life.

A more mundane example is grocery shopping. Ponder what happens if you go to the supermarket without a list of what you want. You wander the supermarket lanes trying to mentally picture what is in the refrigerator — trying to remember if you saw enough milk there. You are annoyed and stressed when you arrive home and realize you forgot the eggs you planned to get. All that stress and mental energy wasted because you did not know what you wanted. Five minutes making a list and you would have saved not only more time, but also your sanity.

Final Prescription

So as the shrink who shrinks problems, not people, let me give you one more prescription (and I'm getting better at living my own prescription). In this busy world that values action more than reflection, take the time to examine the not-so-simple question. Before you rush to judgment or action, check whether *you* are *choosing* what you say or do. Observe whether you are getting what you really want, or settling for what you blindly allow. No one else will be, or should be, focused on getting you what you want. That's your job. But ironically, when you know and go for what you want, they will get what they want. You will have much more freed up energy, creativity and heart to enrich both your life and theirs.

ABOUT DAVID MEE-LEE, M.D.

David Mee-Lee is a physician, a Board-certified psychiatrist and an addictions specialist. He is the "Solutions Psychiatrist" — the Shrink who shrinks problems, not people!

Dr. Mee-Lee is not your usual psychiatrist. He writes and speaks in down-to-earth, jargon-free language to help people understand how to get what they want. David works with corporations, healthcare organizations, schools, county and state agencies to change and cope.

Just because he has had past academic affiliations with Harvard University, University of Hawaii and the University of California in Davis doesn't mean he's snobby and obscure. David's down-to-earth upbringing in Australia coupled with his Chinese heritage makes for an interesting mix of dry humor and quiet wisdom. If you ever hear him speak, you'll enjoy his Aussie accent, but you'll appreciate even more what he says and how he says it.

Contact Information:
David Mee-Lee, M.D.
4228 Boxelder Place
Davis, CA 95616
Phone: (530) 753-4300
Fax: (530) 753-7500
E-mail: info@dmlmd.com
Website: www.DMLMD.com

Designing Boundaries at Work, Home and Play

by Michelle M. Weil, Ph.D.

This chapter is a personal gift for me and you. I could not have completed it at this point in my life without designing and following the boundaries I will describe for you. I can't be authentic unless I practice what I preach, and this chapter is a testimonial to my commitments. I have been practicing the concepts presented in this chapter, along with many others I have taught. They work!

My plan is to hook you so you read the chapter — in whole or in parts. A snapshot of reality will show you how we are all experiencing life today at work, home, and play in less than optimal ways.

Unsteady = Stressful and Nerve Wracking

I want to capture your attention while you're taking in sound new ideas and revisiting solid life concepts, entice you to see yourself and others in my examples, tantalize your brain, and awaken your thinking and creativity! Following this, my aim is to be clear, offer you easily assimilated information, and enhance your desire to put the ideas to use. Right now. In doing so, you can change your unsteady world into an immediately steadier place.

We all need help. That's why self-help books (like this one) are the top sellers. Types of assistance for us all have been developing in better and more acceptable forms since the turn of the century — the 20th that is. Often, we need other people to see our blind spots, because we all have them, and by definition — you guessed it — we are blind to the very things that may influence our most important and fundamental choices.

Today, we live in a world operated by avoidance, denial, and lack of accountability. Our "overwhelms" and stressors have taught us all to "not see" matters of importance because we believe we don't have the time or the information to address the issues.

You deserve the best possible life experience. Life is learning — constantly. This is what makes it challenging, fun, and fascinating. We can choose to see ourselves and our environments as positively ever-changing and ever-growing. Go for the brass ring, today, tomorrow, and every day thereafter. Believe me, you are worth it! If you doubt me, go ask someone who loves you.

As a psychologist and international authority on overcoming stress, I think about the human condition, how to make things better, and about doing what we can to save our sanity, ourselves, our children, and everything we hold near and dear.

Stress affects us all. We share common as well as individualized reactions to stress. Some common reactions (which we might not notice in ourselves) are

- Being overly grouchy; thinking less clearly.
- Processing information more slowly.
- Eating less or more than is good for us.
- Making more impulsive decisions and taking quicker actions.
- Isolating ourselves from others in various ways.
- Using alcohol and prescription medications, along with illegal substances, more readily to dampen and numb distress.
- Blaming others more easily for almost anything that goes wrong.
- Getting angry more quickly and sleeping poorly.

If you aren't sure which ones sound like you, ask your significant others to use the above as a checklist for you. They may see what you can't. It's okay. That's what friends are for. Friends take pleasure in helping keep us in better shape.

Boundaries = Balance and Safety

In these pages, I give you some ways of creating sure footing in the quicksand of life. I will show you how to apply these ideas liberally at work, home, and play. These ideas and "how-to's" set you free to build and use the information as a map or blueprint for a way of living that stabilizes you, your lifestyle, and helps your loved ones, now and forever.

"Knowing is not enough, we must apply.
Willing is not enough, we must do."
— Johann von Goethe

Your positive personal and professional results can be dramatic. The sky is the limit here, and the choice is yours. I hope you use what I offer to make it a great moment, a terrific day, your best year ever, and beyond. Please enjoy this chapter again and again, pass the information along, and create an upward spiral of growth and balance in this unsteady world!

First, we'll look at general information about boundaries and why they are good news for us all. Next, we'll look at examples of today's Boundary Invaders and Boundary Busters. This is "the stuff" that makes life unsteady. You'll quickly get the idea. Then, we'll look at Boundary Building and the ways we can Design Boundaries for Balance at work, home and play.

The Importance of Designing Boundaries

What are boundaries?

A boundary is simply a grown-up version of limit-setting. One way of thinking about boundaries is that we are parenting ourselves as adults and setting limits for ourselves and others with whom we interact. We know from child development experts that healthy children don't show up by accident. They are the product of love and consistent parental limit-setting, both of which give children a sense of belonging and teach them how to be. Clear rewards and consequences teach children accountability for their actions. The best parents and teachers continually reinforce good behavior and take action against inappropriate behavior patterns. When this learning style and attitude toward life is delivered with love and clarity, children flourish.

What do boundaries do for us?

Boundaries give us information. They are like a personal measuring stick or barometer telling us where we stand with someone, when a line is crossed, the difference between right and wrong, or when we or someone else is being honest or dishonest. Boundaries and the information system they create give us the ability to feel mastery in our lives and our relationships. Mastery does not mean we become controlling or rigid, simply clearer and calmer. Remember the map idea? Maps give us options to get from where we are to where we want to go. They provide choices, security, and a plan. We can take as many side trips as we want along the way, and clearly enjoy the ride. But we know our destination point. Internal and external safety is created by establishing and maintaining boundaries.

Why are they necessary?

Boundaries and how they are respected or ignored give us a built-in feedback system. The feedback system helps us decide when to act and what to do. Information about how others react to our boundaries serves as a boundary barometer, letting you know where, what, and who are the boundary busters and boundary respecters at work, home, and play arenas. You can use this feedback, to enhance your personal, professional, and social self. Maintaining boundaries offers you time and space to think, work, be, create, play, dream, and more!

Boundary Invasion

Our Life Is Under Siege

Realistically, life just isn't as safe as it used to be. This thought has been festering in me for quite some time, and I'll bet it has crossed your mind as well. In the past number of years, we have witnessed and experienced the stock market crashing, well-respected businesses becoming corrupt, the tragedy of 9/11, threats and the actualization of war, fears of retaliation, terrorism in our country, and more. During this time, I have watched, listened, and learned more about people and their reactions. What follows are examples that cut across our arenas of work, home and play.

Driving is downright dangerous

We all know drinking and driving don't mix. Does that stop people? No. And what about driving and stress? They don't mix either. Today, people are driving badly — in many more ways than before. You get tailgated, honked at, or flipped off if you dare to drive the speed limit. If the person behind you doesn't want you to make that right-hand turn, you'll surely get their message as you try to slow down, and turn on your right blinker. Even though you do not want to make a "bat turn" by flying around your intended corner, sometimes we feel forced by the cars behind or around us to take evasive action. Did you know they now teach defensive driving to teens? It's no wonder!

Taking an airline flight is mind-boggling

Today, we don't know how many parts of our bodies, carry-ons, tennis shoes, and purses will be searched in the airport, nor how many times. We must get to the airport extraordinarily early and sometimes be bused on or off the tarmac. We are all suspect until proven innocent!

Staying healthy is more complex than carbohydrates

Why Weight? Okay, what is the diet craze of the day? The Zone, grapefruit and egg diet, Sugar Busters, Protein Power, Weight Watchers, Jenny Craig, Atkins . . . and more. Which chart should we read to tell us what our optimal weight is, or should we decide by the fit of our clothes, the Victoria Secret Catalog, or the *Sports Illustrated* Swimsuit Edition?

Fit or Fat? Is it muscle mass versus fat weight, dunk tanks, or pinch testing? Do pounds matter or inches, I forget. Should we be doing aerobics, kick-boxing, walking the dog, weight lifting, *Curves*, stationary cycling in a sweaty room, or mountain biking in the great outdoors? Are couch potatoes better than baked potatoes? Or are they both banned now?

Scanners and Tanners? Well, there are brain scans, mammograms, tread-mill "stress" heart testing, full-body scans, and more to tell us the level of our health and wellness. Or scare us to death. We can have our cholesterol tested, our hormones replaced, and a pinch of testosterone for that extra zip or simply rub Viagra all over our body. Is the tan look in or out? And is the sun good or bad? Which sunscreen do we need? SPF 10, 15, 2000? Or should we simply buy the clothes that are made with the sunscreen built in? Makes me wonder, do they make UV protected skivvies yet?

"There's no place like home." — Dorothy, in the "Wizard of Oz"

Home life and playtime are affected by the way life has changed, too. For many of us, it is no longer an easy decision to let our children go to the movies, the mall, or even a friend's house. Depending on our kid's age, the wiser parents check who has Internet access and what filters or supervisors are at the home their children are going to visit. This insurance is necessary for the chat groups and instant messaging to be a safe play area, along with what the kids do "offline," to stay "in line!"

Many schools no longer give our children lockers because of the drug, alcohol, and weapons scare, so their backpacks are overstuffed with books, and a new age of back problems in the young is in the making. My kids think it's cool that the police bring a trained dog sniffing for drugs at unexpected times on their junior high and high school campuses. I do too. But think about what this says about our society and level of safety!

Dorothy, in the "Wizard of Oz," could click her heels and say, "There's no place like home." But this *is home*, and no clicking of heels makes it magically change. But we can with Boundary Building. Read on!

"Time, Time, Time Is On Our Side, Yes It Is…" —The Rolling Stones

Well, it's about time . . . to look at time. Today, we are all short on time and have many more things to juggle than ever before. Technology promised us more free time, yet actually takes our time in new, unanticipated, and unexpected ways. We are drowning in a world of too much changing and conflicting information and too many techno-toys, techno-tools and techno-choices. This Boundary Invasion is called Information Overload.

Information Overload

People are being buried under an avalanche of spoken, unspoken, and written words. It has been estimated that information in the world doubles or triples in approximately every 70 days. The Library of Congress catalogs more than 10,000 new items every day. "Snail" mail, FedEx, Airborne Express, and junk mail clog our lives. Yet we are told not to believe everything that we read or hear. It is clearly harder to decipher the truth today, and more information is put forth as the truth or fact than ever before.

As technology and communication modalities explode, the overabundance of connection possibilities becomes an additional source of information overload. We have to sort through and filter vast quantities of electronic information today. Thousands of new websites and e-mail addresses are created on a daily basis — many for the same person on different servers. Cell phones, pagers, e-mail, PDA's, DSL lines, wireless remote access, satellite dishes with hundreds of channels, voice mail, call forwarding, call waiting, answering services, complex automated touch-tone systems . . . the list goes on and on. Add into the mix talk shows radio and television — not to mention Howard Stern.

Junk mail, junk e-mail, virus-laden mass mailings sent through the post office and by e-mail, hackers, crashes . . . YIKES! Airborne Express and airborne viruses . . . Gee, is it safe to go outside?

Help

Now, with so many ways to connect, it is actually harder to reach other people. We spend more time trying to connect for less actual connection. Welcome to our world today.

From these life samples and examples, you can see that we live in a constant state of tension and stress and experience Boundary Invasion from a multitude of factors.

Multitasking Madness

As humans, we are good at multitasking — to a point. It is the normal way of keeping a handle on all that life sends our way. We have always worked to stay effective by multitasking. Yet today, we shift too often from task to task, move faster and faster, feel short on time, and actually create a briefer attention span. We are multitasking past our point of capability. This is a sensory Boundary Invasion I call "Multitasking Madness."

What is Multitasking Madness? Today we run around in our work, home, and play arenas with a heightened sensitivity. This level of daily stress, sensory overload, and unsteadiness either keeps us or puts us on "Red Alert" more easily than ever before.

Multitasking madness comes from a variety of sources:

- Internal self-interruption — shifting from one task to the next to the next without finishing any one of them
- External interruptions and distractions caused by technology, noise, and other people
- Our increased exposure to technology's multitasking capabilities and the belief we should be able to keep up
- Overwhelming amounts of e-mail, phone and cell calls, pages, faxes, snail mail, and junk mail to sift and filter every day
- A lack of balance and safety in our daily routines caused by unexpected life events, tragedies, and changes
- Ever-changing jobs, life demands, and health emergencies in ourselves and others
- Unsteady daily life created by known and unknown societal stressors

How much are Information Overload and Multitasking Madness invading your life?

Use this simple Boundary Invasion Checklist to find out.

Are you experiencing any of these? Mark, or count, all that apply to you.

- ☐ Sleeping difficulties of any kind
- ☐ Remembering things "to do," or things you forgot to do, during other activities or sleep
- ☐ Overwhelmed, nervous, more tearful, easily frightened, jumpy

- ☐ Chronic fatigue and exhaustion, cranky, more judgmental of yourself and others
- ☐ Feeling disorganized, losing things, taking longer to finish tasks
- ☐ "To Do" Lists that never get "Ta Done"
- ☐ Forgetfulness
- ☐ Increased general stress, anxiety, and avoidance
- ☐ A strong desire to hide by staying in bed with the covers over your head.
- ☐ Wanting to run away from it all or go to some far away place for a long time
- ☐ Losing track of your point, or thought, even mid-sentence
- ☐ More anxious and/or restless than usual
- ☐ Feeling low, helpless, down, or depressed more often
- ☐ Worse at problem solving than before
- ☐ Job-related, or lack-of-job-related stress
- ☐ Impatient, irritable, angry, frustrated, bored, lonely
- ☐ Resistance and avoidance of things you used to do more easily
- ☐ Stress about raising your kids in general, or about any of these:
    - Daycare issues
    - Teacher attrition and/or teacher overload and burnout
    - School entrance requirements and tuition
    - Academic and extracurricular demands
    - Social cliques and "fitting in"
    - Kids and Technology, access, intrusion and safety, expense
    - Expenses and money
    - Sex, drugs, alcohol, gangs, shootings, suicides

If you are experiencing any of the above, your score is too high. You are on Information Overload and experiencing Multitasking Madness. Recognizing this information about you equates to empowering yourself! You now have a better idea about some of the Boundary Invaders in your life — at work, home and play. Luckily, life does not have to stay this way! We all have a choice, so read on . . .

"Do what you can, with what you have, where you are."
— Theodore Roosevelt

Boundary Building at Work, Home and Play

Think of boundary building as being related to body building. We know that developing stronger muscles adds to our overall stamina, health, and well-being. Building boundaries creates sturdy emotional muscles. You will become flexible, strong, energetic, and assertive as you apply the clarity of new boundaries to your life.

These ideas are for you. You will see that they are applicable to all areas of your daily life. Whether directed to a child, co-worker, spouse, and friend or to you, these boundary builders apply to all.

Boundaries are necessary today more than ever! Why?

Life keeps changing the rules on us, so the internal rules we place on ourselves, others, and life need to become more sturdy and steadfast so we can feel hearty and healthy. Life today is more difficult, stress-filled, scary, and less stable than ever before. It is up to us to do the balancing we need and to take charge of the areas we can. Boundary design and maintenance offer us the opportunity to feel safe, to experience clarity in thinking and in our world view, to trust and feel calm, to focus, and to feel productive, creative, and at our personal best. Caring for ourselves through designing boundaries and respecting them also offers us the time to grow, do our regularly necessary self-maintenance (inner and outer repair work), and to live, work and love optimally. I call this first set of Boundary Builders, "Stop the Madness."

"Living well and beautifully and justly are all one thing."
— Socrates

Stop the Madness

1. Practice staying in the moment and focus on only one thing at a time.
2. Develop a "To Do List" skill that works. Learn how to make a *true* priority list. Create an *essential* and *non-essential*

breakdown of the things you need to do.

3. Make a maximum of three essential items a priority. Three is key. That's all, folks. Don't add another group of three until the first group is done.
4. Maintain your focus on each priority and allow yourself time to complete one task before moving on to anything else.
5. Don't make cell calls while driving. Listen to music, look out the window, or simply focus on the pleasure of safe driving.
6. Break projects down into workable pieces. Give yourself a realistic deadline for each portion and attend only to the one section you are working on at the time. After completing each part, reward yourself.
7. Take breaks! Spend time away from work, technology and other ongoing responsibilities. Don't work 24/7.
8. Take a time-management course or seminar that helps you balance work, home, and play.
9. Teach everyone in your family, at work, and your friends how to stop breaking through each other's boundaries.
10. Reinforce any and all successes and steps forward. Become your own personal cheerleader.

"Oh It's A Great Big Beautiful Tomorrow . . . "

— General Electric's Carousel of Progress,
1964 World's Fair, New York, NY

Well, By Designing Boundaries, It Really Can Be

Now, let's look at how to unload some of the overload. Sounds en"lighten"ing doesn't it? You will have more fun, feel more productive, and have fewer interruptions. You'll be less jumpy too.

Offloading Information Overload

1. Work on human-time. When setting time expectations, add extra for real life to happen. You need time for the inevitable technology crashes, illness, play days, naps, doctor's appointments, sleeping through the alarm, relatives showing up and never leaving, reading this chapter, and many other interrup-

tions.

2. Spend time away from technology. Go outside and do something physical. It helps maintain your sanity and perspective.
3. Whenever possible, shut off cell phones and all the other ringers and buzzers around you at home, work, in your car, at meals, and in the grocery. Don't take them with you when you go out to play.
4. Designate a time to check all voice mails and e-mail. Read and listen only to the priority items, and save the rest for later. Erase and delete as much as possible. Respond only when you have the time, and try not to respond impulsively but reflexively.
5. Don't pile papers and magazines to read later when you "have time." Toss them out. If the information is important down the road, there are many ways to retrieve it.
6. Toss junk mail out immediately, and have one of your kids call all catalogues to take you off mailing lists. Save trees, your sanity, and time!
7. Practice access control. It's like safe sex. Be selective about who has access to you via pager, cell phone, and e-mail.
8. Protect stringently your personal downtime.

Parental Boundary Building

In order to be a more hands-on parent these days, you can design and commit to certain boundaries that will improve your relationship with your children — both immediately and forever after. Use these ideas to catch the wave and then keep surfing with them as you and they grow. You will be amazed at the results.

Your children will grow up, you will like them, they will like you and themselves, they will marry people you like and they love, and they will invite you to their house for dinner.

Here are some parental boundary design ideas to get you started

1. Monitor what your children watch on TV.
2. Monitor what your pre-teens and teens do on the Internet, at home, and at friends' homes.

3. Put time restrictions on technology use and include all forms of technology: Internet, Playstation, Game Cube/X-Box, Game Boy, CD players and other music, telephone, television, and electronic devices.
4. Make family decisions about the types of CDs and games your kids buy, borrow, and trade.
5. Know where your kids are after school and on weekends. Establish a way to access them, or have check-in times when they call you.
6. Stay aware of their academic performance, set acceptable standards, and utilize fair and firm rewards and consequences.
7. Stay on top of their long-term school projects and help them learn to plan the work in stages and keep ahead of the curve time-wise.
8. Set a curfew and bedtime for school and weekend nights.
9. Establish standards about sex, alcohol, drugs, tobacco, and friends. *Make them clear and discuss them often. Solve compliance problems together.*
10. Have an adult present whenever possible to greet children at home or pick up after school.

Boundary Designs for Better Family Life

The following offers additional suggestions to get you started on developing a healthier family life.

- Have family discussions often and ask everyone to voice opinions about new upcoming events, to express feedback regarding other family members' behavior and attitude, to make plans for agreed-upon changes, and to applaud successes.
- Assign regular daily and weekend household chores to everyone living at home. Make them age appropriate and subject to rewards and consequences.
- Create realistic, achievable, and individualized expectations.
- Don't pay for good grades or overpay allowances. Let your children earn extra money or privileges by good behavior,

family and community responsibilities, chores, or neighborhood jobs.
- Don't listen to TV during dinner. Have family dinners together at least three to five times a week.
- Teach your kids to cook several simple meals and ask them to make dinner for the family every so often.
- Practice access control with family members. Let everyone know when you are available and how to connect with you. Tell them when to leave you alone, and whom to go to for any necessary problem-solving during your unavailable times.

Boundary Building with Significant Others

Practice these skills to improve your relationship with a special someone.

- Set a regular time to talk alone for 15 minutes daily, at a minimum, without interruption from phones, children, or doorbells. Compliment each other frequently.
- Monitor how much time you and your significant spend on TV, technology use, and other activities.
- Think about the time and activity choices you make and look at their relationship to creating more closeness and intimacy.
- Set limits and change whatever creates too much separateness, or loneliness, for one or both of you.
- Compromise if you cannot agree. Meet in the middle and see how it goes.
- Strive to go out on a "date night" without your children once a week. Go away overnight at least once a month.
- Take a class or learn a new sport together, and don't let anything interfere!

Friends

"Friends are like sunshine."

— John Hay

Are you aware that friends are an endangered species today? Friendship is another casualty of our overwhelmed out-of-time lives. Yet, we need friends to help us, love us, console us, and boot us in the behind when we need it! Friends and support systems are an essential part of overall life balance and boundary maintenance. Many of us are shy; or, believing that we are unlovable, we are afraid to reach out. But you must do it anyway! There are safe places to practice where you can find good people to connect with.

Making friends doesn't happen overnight. Think of the analogy of learning to walk. You start, you stumble, you start again, you falter, and you keep at it anyway. Why? It is a built-in developmental drive. Eventually, you are running and don't even think about the steps. The need people have for other people is also a built-in developmental drive. Use it to make connections with others.

Make at least three new friends. Remember, three is key. Look into support groups; community centers; adult education classes; and activities at your local community college, churches or synagogues; skills classes and training at pet stores (your dog will appreciate it), home improvement stores, and arts and crafts stores. Ask around town. Check the local newspapers to see what's available.

Go Play

Play is an essential ingredient in our overall well-being, but it often gets lost in a horde of Boundary Invaders. Today, it is necessary for many of us to use the boundary building skills described in this chapter to make and preserve time for play. Make play a commitment to yourself and to your friend(s). Schedule it on your calendar and consider it an appointment. Make it as important to preserve as if you were meeting with the President.

If you have forgotten what you like to do, make a list of things that sound like fun or that you used to like, and try them one at a time. Playtime can be easy to do at home, such as watching the humming birds (you have to fill the feeder), or more involved, such as going on a trip. Ideas on your list can range from simple to complex — solitary or shared experiences — and they can be fun. You choose what works for you. If you are rusty at the skill of fun, it is good to have a friend or loved one to help generate ideas for fun.

Boundary Building with Money

Financial stability is an important ingredient in maintaining balance in an uncertain world. Money is such a big problem area for many of us. It is so big, it deserves an entire book! But I wanted to mention it briefly and alert you to the fact that one of the reasons money can be such a problem is that people don't set clear boundaries regarding money, budgets, the use of credit, and the like.

There are over-spenders just like over-eaters. If we eat too much, we gain weight. If we spend too much, we go into debt.

If you think through the following list, you'll get the idea about where to look in your life and see the need for boundary setting. Yes, the stock market goes up and down, as do real estate prices and our weight, but here are some things we can plan for and stick with, no matter what. And remember, lots of good advice is available today, even at no cost, regarding money matters and financial planning. If you make a decision to address these areas as part of your overall balancing, I promise you, you'll feel safer instead of sorry.

Think through and set limits on:

- budgets
- gadgets
- kids' allowances
- adult allowances — yes, you can give yourself a weekly or monthly play allowance for clothing or entertainment
- monthly, semi-annual, and annual bills
- federal and state taxes
- self-employment taxes

Saving for the unexpected such as:

1. illness
2. job loss
3. divorce
4. moving
5. accidents
6. theft

7. income cut-backs
8. emergencies

Boundary Backfires

Why might putting these ideas to work be difficult for you?

I have worked with people of all types and from all walks of life, helping them create change for more than 25 years. One thing is certain. When you grow in ways that others aren't used to, there is often a period of disruption, or backfire. Now that you will be practicing the skills of boundary building and boundary setting, those around you may squirm.

However, let me assure you of this: If it is good for you, and you become a happier person, the people around you will feel the change and be just fine. For instance, if co-workers are used to you as a "yes-person" who then procrastinates, they have felt the frustration of your not meeting deadlines. However, when you begin to set clearer boundaries and realistic deadlines, the same co-workers may be taken aback for a bit, but will be delighted to experience you doing what you said you would do — and on time.

The same goes for your kids and significant others. As you set limits, they may rebel a bit. However, please explain why you are making the changes, and ask them to do the same (or have them read this chapter with you). Overall, they will experience you as being more *present* when you are with them, and they will feel happier with you than before.

"Happiness depends upon ourselves."

— Aristotle

If you find that, after putting some effort into implementing these ideas, you aren't as successful as would like, get some assistance. There are many ways to garner self-improvement: seminars, books (like this one), personal coaching, spiritual guidance, 12-step growth groups (on every kind of life issue), individual, family, and group therapy and counseling, and many other support and self-help groups.

Societal Boundary Building

When I was a child in elementary school I learned to "duck and cover" and to "stop, drop and roll." Those are two of the drills we were taught to protect ourselves in case of an emergency. The following ideas describe some new drills and ways to protect ourselves and our society today.

Think about this

Our work commute has now become downright hazardous to our physical and emotional health. Since the beginning of 2003, I have seen some tragic, horrific accidents. Today there are more car accidents, fender-benders, and serious multi-vehicle crashes. I believe these accidents, in part, are due to our mounting stress and how we are choosing to react.

As the saying goes, "rain happens," and we need to slow down. But, we don't! The other day, on my way home, after witnessing yet another tragic accident on the Interstate, and watching the other cars carelessly speeding around the scene, to get wherever, faster . . . the Boundary Building mantra "Stop, Breathe, and Think" came to mind as a more realistic drill for us today. First, let's look at the application of this phrase and where we can put it to good use.

Societal "Owies" We Create and Their Solutions

In general, people are behaving badly, and in places where they did not do so before. We have become less courteous and thoughtful. Yep, you, me, and all the rest of us. And yes, there *are* lots of reasons. Regardless, I believe it's time to "Stop, Breathe, and Think." Without realizing it, we are all adding to our life stress. Each and every one of us, every day. We are generally more nervous and jittery because it is a tough time to be alive. This is true whether you are five years old, fifty years old, or 500 years old; and all the ages I have missed in between.

Let's stop doing what we are doing that adds to the stress by following a few simple checkpoints inside and outside ourselves and in those around us. We need to slow down and think problems and behaviors all the way through. The following lists are some ways to avoid creating additional stress and potential tragedies.

"The superior man is modest in his speech, but excels in his actions."

— Confucius

If you are participating in any of the following behaviors, "Stop, Breathe, and Think"

- Tailgating or fast lane changes while driving. These are downright dangerous and cause every driver around to be extra nervous.
- Cheating others in any way at work or in your business, or not being honest.
- Not doing your very best at your job of parenting, work, or with your friends and family.
- Getting angry at traffic accidents on the highways that cause a back-up in commute time. Seriously think about this one, and be thankful the accident doesn't involve you or someone you love. But remember, it does involve someone loved.
- Over-reliance on technology, and/or thinking it is foolproof.
- Flipping people off (or reasonable facsimiles of that behavior) because they are slowing down to make a left or right turn in front of you. Remember, you need to turn too, sometimes.
- Not saying "I'm sorry" enough. This is so powerful and under-utilized!
- Yelling at your kids as they go through their version of "acting out normally" due to their current experience of the world and how it touches their lives.
- Going above the speed limit, and not keeping double the safe distance between you and the car ahead of you — triple it, if weather conditions aren't optimal.

"Duck and cover" and all the other safety drills won't cut it anymore. What we have learned is the following: Wars, global disasters, terrorism, national and international threats = Societal Stress and Worldwide Boundary Invasion.

So, let's get growing! It is the best way to empower ourselves and steady our lives and ourselves. We need to take a different type of action, one that is proactive, not passive and protective. These Boundary Builders will cut across work, home and play.

"Adopt the pace of nature, her secret is patience."
— Ralph Waldo Emerson

Societal Boundary Building for Balance

Here's what *we can* do:

- Don't take things personally; others are stressed, too. Be accepting and forgiving.
- Allow each frightening moment, no matter how disruptive, to remind you that we are a global community. We need to help each other now, more than ever.
- Do things that soothe you more often. Schedule them in.
- Talk to others about your true feelings and *really* listen to theirs. This is an amazing de-stressor. When you listen with care, miracles can happen.
- Recognize and appreciate the support and the outpouring of helpful information.
- Behave in a more civilized manner, and with enhanced dignity and integrity. Work at this!
- Believe there will always be more good in life than bad, and acknowledge that you can make a difference.
- Remember, this is both a new adventure and a new era that we are all experiencing together. We clearly can't predict all the bumps, potholes, or curves ahead. We can, however, take charge of our actions and thoughts and enjoy the journey with our eyes open and our hearts at peace. To do so, it is imperative we behave our best and feel good about ourselves.

"The right to happiness is fundamental."
— Anna Pavola

ABOUT MICHELLE M. WEIL, PH.D.

Dr. Michelle Weil is a Professional Keynote Speaker, Corporate Consultant, Clinical Psychologist, the Miss Manners of Technology and author of the books TechnoStress: Coping With Technology @Work @Home @Play, *which teaches you how to thrive in the age of high-tech, and* The Mental Health Technology Bible. *From "Good Morning America" to the* Wall Street Journal, *she is sought after for her commentary on resolving the stress that is created in our lives. Dr. Weil is a constant author in professional and popular journals and magazines. She was recently interviewed by the* San Diego Tribune, *authored "Rx for TechnoStress" in NSA's* Professional Speaker *magazine (May 2003), published the article entitled "Stop, Breathe and Think — It's Time," in the* National Psychologist *(July/August, 2003), and was honored by being asked to be the closing Keynote at the prestigious American Community Preparedness Conference in Louisville, KY in October 2003. Through extensive media coverage along with her role as National Spokesperson for MCI, Activision and others, Dr. Weil has reached millions with her message and her wisdom. She heads the consulting firm Human-Ware, LLC, www.human-ware.com, is an avid speaker, trainer and writer, maintains a private clinical psychology practice, and is the mother of two children and two stepchildren.*

Contact Information:
Michelle M. Weil, Ph.D.
Human-Ware, LLC
Phone: (760) 730-3894
Website: www.Human-Ware.com
E-Mail: Weil@Human-Ware.com

Recapturing Balance When Your World Turns Upside Down

---

by Valla Dana Fotiades, M.Ed.

How does one go about recapturing balance when your world turns upside down? We live in a world of constant change. Moment to moment our lives are evolving with the unpredictable encounters that fall into our pathway of life.

Often, when we are tossed into a time of massive change, there will be unstable time before we are able to recapture balance.

Companies downsize. Incredibly talented people are "let go." Companies transfer employees to new locations. Accidents steal lives. Illnesses change life circumstances. Loss of a life-long relationship can be devastating. Sometimes people relocate because parents are getting older and their health could be getting more fragile. It could be that you have had some shocking news about your own health, or you learn that your employment contract is not going to be renewed.

In my case, a seven-year contract, which incorporated health benefits, was cut short. Being a solo mom of two still living at home, I had to make some life-changing decisions.

All of a sudden, you may be searching for new insurance, health care professionals, shopping areas, dentists, places of entertainment, an accountant, organizations to connect with, places of worship, the best schools for your children, a new financial institution to work with, a new post office. New numbers here, strange faces there, and you will experience a multitude of changes everywhere.

When you feel like the fourth leg of your table has been knocked out from under you, here is just a sample of the symptoms you may experience:

- feeling sick in your stomach
- having little or no appetite
- feeling as if the air had been knocked out of you
- experiencing food tasting like cardboard even when it is heavily spiced
- feeling like curling up in a tight little ball and sleeping when normally you would be jumping out of bed to anxiously embrace what the new day has to offer
- feeling depressed and/or anxious
- feeling angry at others for creating your situation
- sleeping without getting a good rest
- feeling disjointed and unable to concentrate and focus

How do you continue to function?

Let me share a couple of stories to show you what different people have done to work through these difficult bumps of change.

A colleague of mine in the National Speakers Association was downsized from his international corporation. He had traveled extensively throughout the world, was well-received in his profession and found himself sitting in a temporary office, with office equipment and business cards, provided by his company to give him a six-month opportunity to locate a new job.

He decided to use that time to begin his own consulting and speaking business. It took a few years before it was really doing well. He did say that had he not been forced to look at other opportunities, he may never have had the courage to step out and open his own business.

Change causes us to do some deep soul searching and often to try new experiences that may not have been in our thoughts previously. As I mentioned before, recapturing balance may take a very different amount of time for each individual, depending on the type of change/loss involved.

May 22, 2000, changed my life forever. I was no longer a wife; I was no longer the mediator; I became the sole disciplinarian; I became the sole provider, I became the chief decision maker; I was the head of the household, in charge of all taxes, finances, and repairs. When someone in your life dies suddenly, there is a tremendous amount of adjusting to do.

What I have realized is that everyone handles massive change with a different set of skills. Some people keep themselves so busy they do not have time to think. Sometimes people get very blocked and are not able to function at a normal level/pace. The intensity of the relationship/loss will greatly affect the way people are able to move on. How long may this last? Who knows?

Between March and May of 2000, we lost three friends and two family members. My husband dropped dead eight days after he gave the eulogy for his good golf buddy, who died from a quick cancer, only 41 days after his younger brother had dropped dead. I was afraid to answer my phone wondering what the next message would be.

I had never been to a counselor in my life, but I did go. I would suggest to seek out someone who may have had a similar experience and who you blend with because you may go through several counselors before you find someone who may be able to help you. Some people may work with a counselor for years while others may find it something to do for a short while. The best thing the counselor shared with me was the idea of *Where are you on this scale?* She asked me where I would place myself on a scale of 1-10 if 1 was in bed, curled up in fetal position, unable to eat, unable to sleep and 10 was feeling, not necessarily yourself, but okay. I think I placed myself around 5. When I asked my kids, they placed me at 6. That was a relief to my very stressed and depressed mind.

Another suggestion would be to find an appropriate support group. It took five months before I ventured into a support group for widows and widowers. My friend Pattie and I met in the parking lot and walked in together. Again, I would say, this is something to try. Some of the group members were still coming three years later. When I asked them why, they responded that they wanted to give back and share hope that life would go on again. They did explain that it would be different, but it would go on.

I would also recommend sharing your feelings with your friends. A few months after my husband died, I shared with a good friend how difficult Friday evenings were. Everyone else was going home to share the weekend with his/her mate and it was a difficult time. My friend Chris had the insight to suggest we do a craft evening every Friday because her husband was busy refereeing. Four of us would meet — one married, one single and Pattie, whose husband, the golf buddy, died 11 days before my husband did. We ended up doing this for over seven months and it was extremely helpful during this transition period of learning to be on our own.

At the six-month time, I was able to gather myself together and take part in a yoga class. I found that yoga relaxation was the only thing that cleared my mind, provided total relaxation for a short time, and reduced my stress.

About eight months after I lost my husband, I approached the health care company where I hosted a TV show and offered an idea for a program to help people who had experienced loss. They offered a staff person, a social worker with a lot of experience with loss, and the space. It was my job to find the money necessary to fund this eight-week adventure. I approached the funeral director we had used too often in the last few years and asked if he would be willing to help us help the living! He gave us a check for $1600 to fund the basics for the program and my friend, Pattie, found two other funeral homes that offered small donations that allowed us the opportunity to offer this program to the general public for a very reasonable fee of $40 per person for the eight weeks.

It was exciting. We had greeters and did some fun sharing at the open and close of each program, but never did find out why people had chosen to come to the program, "*Take Time To Breathe, To Renew and Grow Through Your Grief.*"

We offered a smorgasbord of topics, including At the Heart of Wellness, Relax with Massage, Working with Greens and Flowers, Growing Through Life Changes, Tai Chi, Yoga, Cooking for Fewer or One, and ended with an evening of international folk dancing.

These programs were held on a Friday night and were very well-received by the attendees. When it was over, it was hard to readjust to Friday nights.

September 11th happened and our lives changed yet again. I lived in Worcester, MA at the time. We knew a couple of families who were directly hit by this horrific tragedy. I spearheaded a program at my church on "*How to Deal with Loss.*" The speakers included a father whose estranged son had gone down with the first plane into the towers. He shared his story of this sadness. A woman who had been living with cancer, beating it against the odds for over ten years, shared techniques for maintaining hope in times of loss and change. We had a young woman explain the loss of her 31-day-old infant to an unusual illness. People started talking about loss. We opened the pathways and provided opportunities for people to be able to discuss these situations. Provide opportunities for open discussion. This is so critical for all of us to be able to do.

I heard a grief specialist, Dr. Alan Wolfelt, speak last year. He told us that, *"America is the only place where people think death is optional."* And I would add that most people are not willing to talk about it. People are uncomfortable with something they don't usually have much experience with.

What I found was that I never knew so many people were touched by loss until it happened to our family. I ended up gathering a group of young widows together to have a potluck dinner once a month. This full evening of fun and laughter nurtured everyone's soul.

From this group we created a subgroup of parents with children still at home. We called it the Parent Pow-Wow. It gave us the opportunity to meet on a Saturday once a month to discuss childrearing issues, curfews, allowances, clothes allowances and a lot of other ideas that were important when one parent does not have a sounding board to help make decisions on these types of issues.

Many of these women wrote for a booklet (still in progress), *"Tips for Widows on How to Survive the First Year after Loss."* And some of these women participated in a project I spearheaded from the Heart of Massachusetts to the Heart of the Survivors (loved ones left from 9/11). We created five, half-hour videotapes titled *"Life After*

Loss — Learning to Let Your Heart Sing Again."

We were able to deliver 36 of these gift packages to the Family Assistance Center in NYC on May 4, 2002. It was a very exciting mission to be able to offer help to so many people who had experienced such tragic loss.

I mentioned before that on May 22, 2000, my life changed forever. My husband and I were raking our back lawn and then he was gone. Realizing that we are only one breath away from being somewhere else (frightening if we were to dwell on this), would probably make most people a little bit crazy.

The grieving process goes on like a roller coaster, probably forever. Personally, I do not think the old saying, time heals, is accurate. What I do think, from over three years of living this process, is that time distances our intensity of feeling. This loss will always be a part of our life and we will be different. One of my friends, Helen, who was seven years old when her baby sister died said, " You will feel joy again, but it will be a different kind of joy."

Are we prepared when loss or change touches our lives? Since the death of my husband, I have been asked to speak on *"How to Survive Personal Loss/ How To Prepare For Personal Loss."* Well, I did a bit of research interviewing several young widows to see how their experiences compared to mine. It is not that we want to live in a "What if?" mode, but to be realistic about life. We do not know what tomorrow may toss in our life path. I would like to share with you ideas that we found to be very important, to be aware of, think about, and discuss.

#1 — A top priority is life insurance. Do you have enough to be able to pay off your mortgage, buy a new car, help put your children through school, pay for the funeral expenses, and cover the cost of health insurance?

#2 — Is everything you own in joint names? You may do this with a spouse or even a parent, a child or a sibling. Whatever situation you are in, think about joint names for house, vehicles, bank accounts, leased car, Custodian Accounts with children WROS (with right of survivorship). This creates a simple transfer of ownership in the event of death.

#3 — Do you have a will in order? If you have under-age children and something should happen to you and your spouse at the same time, have you arranged for guardians?

#4 — Have you completed your Health Care Proxy? Speak to your medical professional about this. My husband dropped dead at 53. His brother died at 51 — 41 days earlier. My friend's husband was 43, another was 37 and yet another 35. One of these women, who was in the hospital with her husband who was dying of cancer, mentioned how important it is to have the DNR (Do Not Resuscitate) order in place. Remember we do not have any guarantees for where, when, or how we may end up.

#5 — Think about cross-training. What does that mean? Would you know the answers to the following if something happened to your significant other?

- Do you know about all the financial information, bank account numbers, PIN numbers?
- Do you know about all the investments?
- Do you know how to do the taxes or where to go if you need assistance?
- Do you know how much it costs to run your household? Would you be able to run it on one salary?
- Do you know how to put your fingertips on important documents?
- Do you have a filing system that you are both aware of?
- Do you know what kind of arrangements should be made if you were to suddenly depart? Where do you want to be buried? What is your decision concerning burial or cremation? If you are going to be buried, what kind of a headstone do you want? Whose name and information or details will go on that stone?
- Do you have a list of all of your significant other's close friends and business associates, the lawyer, the accountant?
- Do you know each other's passwords for the computer? Do you know where the back-up disks are in case of computer crash?

These little things can throw your mind right over the edge when you are under such tremendous stress.

Where do you go from here? Know that the process of loss is different for everyone. There is no set timetable for "getting over it." I would say it is a roller coaster of emotion, packed full of ups and downs, running at its own pace. When you are in an "up," be sure to take advantage of it.

The last ideas I would like to share with you are suggestions for what to do when someone you know suffers a loss.

1. It is really hard when you don't know what to say. Whether you are in person or over the phone, I have learned to say, "Hi, just wanted you to know that I have been thinking about you." Pause. Be quiet and wait. Give the receiver the gift of your ears to listen.
2. Invite someone over on a regular basis: for an evening of talk, to go for a walk, to share a meal, play a game, enjoy a tea or a simple, relaxing visit. When I was in high school, a friend's mom was ill with cancer, and my mother invited him to our home for a family meal every Wednesday night for a whole year. This was something we all looked forward to, and he enjoyed the pleasant, family time.
3. Call a day ahead and tell someone that you will be coming with dinner, and plan to keep them company for a couple of hours.
4. Call and invite the person to attend a play, a movie, or a concert with you. It is so important to keep involved, yet people often go into withdrawal and isolate themselves.
5. Send someone a thoughtful, handwritten note. I appreciated these notes so much when someone took the time to actually share personal thoughts with me. Many people would write, "Call me," and then sign only a first name. Suggestion! If you really want that person to call you, write your full name and phone number next to your signature. Send a note even if it is a month or two or three later, it will be greatly appreciated.
6. Call someone on a regular basis to check in. Your family can be a great resource. Both my mom and my mother-in-law were getting calls from me daily and sometimes even more than once a day. They were great listeners and a lifeline of hope for me.

7. Be patient. Know that everyone heals in a unique way in their own time frame. Avoid judging someone's space for healing. Be kind, and you will be a wonderful friend in time of loss and change.
8. Encourage someone to write in a journal. I have found that writing my thoughts on paper is very healing, and journaling helps me focus and think more clearly.

Not too long ago, I heard the President of Mass Bay Community College speak. He said, *"Change is inevitable, growth is optional."* When we face changes in our lives, this is a good thought to ponder to help us move on to recapture balance. Another quote I found over the last couple of years that really spoke to this situation is, *"We must be willing to let go of the life we had planned in order to embrace the life that awaits us."*

As we all move forward to our new life experiences, I hope that some of the ideas shared in this chapter will give you tools for understanding when you experience life changes/life losses. I would also hope that the next time you are in the presence of someone who has sustained some type of change/loss that you will think about these ideas and have greater insight for what to do and how to offer some help.

Embrace the journey and remember to nurture yourself when you need to recapture your balance.

ABOUT VALLA DANA FOTIADES, M.ED.

Valla Dana Fotiades, M.Ed., is a Spirit Revitalizer, a consultant, an author and a TV Host of the 5-part series, "Life After Loss: Learning to Let Your Heart Sing Again". Valla hosted the TV Talk Show, "For Your Health," for 7-1/2 years, has been an adjunct professor of Speech Communications, and a professional speaker since 1992. She is a past president of the New England Speakers Association and a co-author of two books, Teaching & Joy *and* Exceptional Accomplishment. *She works with individuals and organizations desiring to learn fresh techniques for revitalizing & energizing, and using effective skills for communicating and presenting. Clients from different industries offer comments such as, "Great ideas that are practical, inexpensive and applicable. They work!" "It gave me redirection in my life." "A joyous learning experience!" "I'm still smiling at work!!! And still working at smiling!!!" "It is absolutely the most contagious epidemic I have ever had the pleasure of starting!" Currently, Valla is the Comprehensive Health Specialist for the Polk County, Florida, School Board.*

Contact Information:
Valla Dana Fotiades, M.Ed.
Energize Your Life!
P.O. Box 133
Waverly, FL 33877-0133
Phone: (863) 875-0759
Fax: (863) 324-7558
E-mail: Valladana@cs.com

Creating Balance

by Peggy Farmer, Ph.D.

Stop, look, and listen to your life. Are you juggling home, career, family, and community but neglecting your spirit? Are the pieces of your puzzle out of whack?

Some workers clock in for more than 60 hours a week, while chaos runs rampant on the home front. I am currently providing executive coaching for a middle manager in a large multinational corporation. He averages 60 to 80 hours a week at work, sits on the board of his church, coaches his son's soccer team at school, and wonders why he is exhausted at the end of the day. Are we running our lives or are our lives running us? Too often, external demands dictate our schedules. We all need a system that creates order in our lives. Regaining balance requires courage. We constantly have to sift through mail, e-mail, phone calls, reports, bills and other items that all clamor for our attention. We need to filter this flood of information that inundates us daily.

There is a reason for the popularity of the phrase "simplify, simplify, simplify." Put it into practice and the outcome is profound. But therein lies the problem; how do we realistically simplify our lives in a technocratic society, which almost compels us to complicate our lives with the newest "must have" gadget? A person who does not possess a cellular phone is now in the minority, whereas even five years ago, only business people owned them. Simplifying our lives means removing inordinate amounts of stress from our day-to-day existence. Do you really need 80 movie channels and that big house? Do you need dozens of magazine subscriptions instead of just your favorite? Why not get rid of all but one credit card to minimize debt, paper work, stress, and temptation? If we are not careful, our possessions become our burdens.

"Fortunate, indeed, is the man who takes exactly the right measure of himself, and holds a just balance between what he can acquire and what he can use."

— Peter Mere Latham

When we are in balance we receive the gift of a centered mind. When we are out of balance, no matter how much we want to serve, our clarity will be lacking. Balance is critical to optimal wellness.

The four main areas of our overall wellness are body, mind, spirit and service. Examine these four areas of your life. Consider how much time you contribute to each. How do you feed your body? Are you eating healthy foods that support your well-being? Preparing a healthy meal with the help of family members can take 10 minutes, which is less time than it would take to stop for take-out at the local restaurant — and much more beneficial for all.

Are you doing some form of exercise that you love and that feels good to you? Lack of time is often the main reason or excuse that people use for not exercising. I have found with many clients that the problem goes deeper. We often do not do things that we don't want to do; we will resist, put off, and avoid exercise as if it were the plague. A simple solution is to find ways to move your body that you actually enjoy! How about five minutes of gentle stretching in the morning to awaken your joints and prepare your body for a day of fluid movement? Why not spend five minutes in the evening dancing to your favorite song? Research has shown that even 10 or 15 minutes of moderate exercise is all you need to keep you in balance.

Do you pamper your body with hot baths, massage, or the luxury of sleeping in? Balance comes from within, and honoring your body when it is tired will go a long way towards remaining well for the long haul. Massage relieves the tension in your muscles and restores a sense of homeostasis within the body.

Are you feeding your mind and intellect stimulating thoughts that sharpen your mental clarity? Are you keeping good company instead of surrounding yourself with negative influences that drain your energy and stifle your creativity? Feeding the mind does not require strenuous mental exercise; simply challenge yourself to think new thoughts that uplift you. Challenge yourself to think in new, creative ways. Seek out people that you don't know and begin a conversation to expand your horizons.

Is your spirit being fed by nature, silence, love, sweetness and solitude? Do you allow yourself quiet time to reflect on the mysteries of creation, the flowers, the animals, the magnificent sky, and the endless ocean? Is your spirit nourished or malnourished? Do you read uplifting books and study various subjects to maintain your mental health?

Do you value service? What steps are you taking to share your resources with others? Do you reach out beyond your self-imposed comfort zones to serve the world through your work? Perhaps you are spending too much time serving others and neglecting yourself. A pivotal point in the balance equation is calculating the appropriate measure between service to self and service to others. Each must be carefully assessed and balanced to avoid being too egocentric or too selfless.

No discussion of balance would be complete without a cursory glance at the motivation to create balance in our lives. One must be willing to create a life of balance because of a desire to live a life of purpose. Often our intentions are noble, but our behavior doesn't reflect them; to live your life on purpose is to make a bridge between behavior and intentions. Why aren't our intentions always mirrored in our actions? The answer is that often our spoken intentions are not our heartfelt truths or deepest desires. Are your career goals based on what you thought your parents or friends felt would be most advantageous for you? Do we make the connection between our thoughts, words, actions, internal motivations, and intentions?

To answer these questions we have to increase our self-awareness and deeply explore our inner landscape. What are my intentions in life? What do I want to accomplish with my life? Am I living my life on purpose based on my mission statement or on someone else's vision? Did you want to be an artist but were told to be an engineer?

Did you long to be an oceanographer but were persuaded to be an accountant? By exploring our intentions we can consciously make decisions consistent with our personal and professional goals and core values. Our core values guide our path and keep us on track. Aligning values with intention equals freedom from stress. If you know your purpose, align it with your values and act on your intentions. The result of this practice will be a life lived on purpose, and the stress of wondering what your life is all about or what to do with your life will be a concern of the past. Intentionality has several aspects, including managing distractions and remaining focused on objectives. Why do we procrastinate? Why do we tackle the easy stuff first and leave the hard stuff for later? Either we're not fully committed or we haven't transformed commitment to conviction.

There is an urgency that comes with living your life on purpose, a passion to act on your heartfelt desires and make your visions a reality. Unwavering focus allows us to get what we want, and focus comes from quieting the mind and zeroing in on stated intentions to come up with an action plan. Then we need the courage to step out confidently among our peers and let our convictions lead to fruition.

Another aspect of intentionality lies in our ability to be aware of our internal motivations. Are there ulterior motives when we seek certain friendships or partnerships? Do we have unspoken expectations and unspoken motives that complicate our relationships and hinder our ability to be successful in our stated intention?

The opposite of intentionality is impulsiveness, randomly behaving haphazardly without thinking of the consequences of our actions. Don't confuse impulsiveness with spontaneity. When we act with intentionality, we accept responsibility for both our actions and motivations. Balance requires that we be willing to live life on purpose and align our intentions with our desire to restore a sense of harmony in our everyday lives.

Let these questions and suggestions promote a guilt-free, shameless self-inquiry. Use them to perform exploratory surgery of your soul and uncover where you are losing energy. Find your balance "leaks" in the craft of your inner self, make the necessary course corrections, and judiciously guide yourself back into balance within the safe harbor of your soul.

Ultimately, we need to balance action with reflection, head with heart, work with play, masculine with feminine, truth with compassion, and love with wisdom. We need to listen again to that quiet voice within. We must reunite all the myriad parts of ourselves into wholeness. We need to realign and reunite our masculine and feminine energies within and shine the light of love on our shadow side. We need to continually remind ourselves to stop searching outside for validation of self-love, self-worth, or a sense of belonging. Each of us has within us all the required tools, skills, and wisdom to be happy, abundant, healthy, balanced, successful, and fully conscious spiritual beings. Most of our young lives we were taught that we were inferior if we did not meet the criteria of the teachers, peer group, or parents' ideas of what it meant to be successful. We have been basing our sense of self-worth on outside sources or prescribed measurements, such as grades, athletic skills, and other markers of achievement, which we mistook for a complete reflection of our self-worth. Balance within comes from an accurate self-assessment and a comprehensive vision of ourselves that includes not only our intellectual or athletic abilities but also our emotional intelligence. Enlightenment is not out there somewhere; it is within you. We simply need to rediscover our inner beauty, our inner wisdom, and to stop separating our true intentions from our behavior.

Examine all the areas of your life that are out of balance. Where there is disharmony and disunity, allow the light of your Higher Self to gently guide you to those areas that need attention. By integrating our inner selves and embracing all parts of ourselves we can then restore balance to the whole self. Achieving balance creates a state of wholeness, unshakeability, and equanimity.

Exploratory Questions for Creating Balance

1. Do I balance work and play?
2. Am I spending quality time with my family?
3. What do I do to keep myself in balance, for example, massages, hot baths, family night out?
4. Am I spending quality time with myself without feeling guilty?
5. Have I integrated my masculine and feminine sides and balanced my shadow side with my light side so that I feel whole inside and out?

"What I dream of is an art of balance, of purity and serenity devoid of troubling or depressing subject matter . . . a soothing, calming influence on the mind, something like a good armchair which provides relaxation from physical fatigue."

— Henri Matisse

ABOUT PEGGY FARMER, PH.D.

Dr. Peggy Farmer is an internationally known speaker, wellness consultant and facilitator with a passion for self empowerment and total well-being. She is the North American Director of Self Mastery International, an organization committed to promoting pathways to personal and organiztional effectiveness. Dr. Farmer delves deeply into the heart of issues so individuals and organizations can co-create innovative, practical solutions to challenges in the workplace. She facilitates women's wellness retreats, couples retreats and corporate retreats. Dr. Farmer writes for national magazines and has recently completed her first book titled Exploratory Surgery for the Soul, A Journey to Self Mastery. *She has produced relaxation tapes, a guided imagery video and is working on her next book,* The ABC's of Self Mastery. *Combing her expertise in psychology, health care and wellness, Dr. Farmer assists individuals and companies to achieve synergy by focusing on compassionate communication, stress reduction techniques and the ability to adapt to change. Known for enthusiasm and high energy, she creates an atmosphere where learning is fun and interactive as well as thought provoking and life transforming .*

Contact Information:
Peggy Farmer, Ph.D.
Self Mastery International
373 Landrum Road
Tryon, NC 28782
Phone: (828) 863-4681
E-mail: pfarmer@teleplex.net
Website: www.selfmasteryintl.com

The Mental Mini-Vacation

by C. Roy Hunter, M.S.

How often do we let stress get the best of us? Have you ever tried to stay calm when people push your buttons, only to find your subconscious taking control? The *Mental Mini-Vacation* may become your key to staying calm in a sea of stress!

This chapter presents a simple technique taught to my clients and audiences over the years. Most clients learning this stress coping skill report varying degrees of help, while some clients enjoy *profound* benefits. For example, any businessperson or salesperson working with clients (or customers) may realize an increased income by staying calm and focused while overcoming objections. Mastering this mental exercise may easily provide benefits to you personally, socially, and professionally.

What Is It?

The Mental Mini-Vacation involves constructive use of the imagination to fantasize an ideal, peaceful place. While doing so, we may establish a "peaceful place" trigger as a reminder to stay calm when our buttons get pushed. The technique is easy to learn and easy to use!

Over the years I have applied various names to the technique. Many clients prefer to call it a form of meditation. Often I refer to it as a self-hypnosis exercise. A 10-minute audiotape based on this technique is entitled, "The 10-Minute Mindpower Nap." Some people call it *creative daydreaming* or *mental imagery*. The technique requires that you take a few minutes several times weekly to sit quietly and go into your imagination — either in a meditative or calm state of mind as much as is possible. This chapter will describe how later.

Why Learn It?

Often we react too quickly to stress and end up dealing with the consequences. We must navigate carefully through stormy seas of stress in this fast-paced society. I often tell audiences: "Today we have the three C's: children, customers, and complainers. If you can stay calm around the three C's, one of the three T's might get you: teenagers, traffic jams, and telephones."

There are many opportunities for others to push our buttons, and the subconscious tends to react in accordance with previous programming. The subconscious is our *mental* computer and must be *programmed* to allow us to maintain self-control in order to avoid reacting without thinking. Whenever willpower and imagination are in conflict, the imagination usually wins out. Many smokers trying to quit demonstrate this fact daily around the country, as well as millions of dieters who keep finding the pounds they lose . . . *why?* The primary reason involves the combination of subconscious programming and the power of the imagination.

Imagination is the language of the subconscious. To demonstrate this to yourself, hold your arms out in front of you, close your eyes, and *imagine* that you hold a bucket in one hand and 100 helium balloons in the other hand. Imagine water pouring into the bucket . . . *see* the water, *hear* it splashing, and *feel* the bucket getting heavier and heavier. Also imagine the helium balloons holding up the other hand, and in less than a minute most people notice a difference between their two arms. This exercise demonstrates the power of imagination!

The negative inhibiting power of imagination can easily be demonstrated by someone whose phobia is activated — whether by heights, elevators, dogs, deep water or spiders, etc. For example, some very intelligent people experience extreme discomfort even looking at a picture of a snake! While the logical mind knows that it is only a picture on a page, the imagination works overtime, causing a discomfort that triggers an immediate emotional reaction.

Lest you doubt the power of your own imagination, ask yourself a simple question: Would you walk comfortably across a one-foot-wide plank between the twin towers of two tall buildings? How much easier would it be to walk that same plank if it were only one inch off the ground? The only difference is the penalty of failure, which would cause the imagination to work overtime.

Mastering the mental mini-vacation will enable you to signal your subconscious to react the way you wish whenever you give yourself a signal activating your new mental program. Incorporated into the technique is what I call *"the peaceful place trigger."* When others push your buttons, they trigger an emotional reaction. Rather than trying to stuff the feelings, simply use your *peaceful place trigger* as a signal to remain calm. To enable this trigger to work, we must change the programming of the inner mind.

How Do We Program the Subconscious?

Since imagination is the language of the subconscious, we must learn to control the imagination and use imagery to reprogram the inner mind. This process is more easily accomplished in a calm state of mind than during times of emotional stress.

Many thousands of hypnotherapists around the world help clients to relax and use their imaginations in positive ways, but most of us can learn to handle stress better simply by learning how to change the subconscious programming on our own. Self-hypnosis is actually meditation with a focus (as opposed to blanking out your mind).

If you do not like to call it self-hypnosis, that's fine. Many trainers teaching forms of meditation prefer to use other names in order to make it more palatable to their audiences. We may also call it mental imagery, regardless of which of the five senses we imagine. During a meditative (or relaxed) state of mind, we can fantasize more vividly.

Some clients tell me, "I don't visualize." Usually these same people can imagine the sound of a waterfall, or the feel of a pet, or warm sand beneath bare feet, etc. Certainly we all have the ability to fantasize the taste of our favorite foods; just ask the person trying to stay on a diet whether or not this is true!

Before you begin, set aside a few minutes when you will be uninterrupted. I personally find it helpful to have soft music playing in the background to drown out outside noise and to help me focus on my peaceful place.

Doing It . . .

Find a comfortable place to relax: seated, reclined, or lying down. With your eyes closed, take several deep breaths and tell yourself to relax. Imagine an ideal, peaceful, and pleasant place. Fantasize a relaxing feeling entering your feet, and moving up through your entire body. Some people enjoy fantasizing a Jacuzzi, while others prefer to simply imagine lying in the sun (or under the shade of a tree).

Your imagination is like the "holodeck" of your mind, where you can move through time and space and create any reality you desire. However, for programming your peaceful place trigger, it's best to imagine a private place of tranquility and beauty. It can be a real place from your past, a place you've seen in magazines or movies, or a fictitious place that exists only in your imagination.

You may use the sample script reprinted below from my self-hypnosis book, *Master the Power of Self-Hypnosis* (Sterling Publishing, 1998). Modify it as needed. I suggest that you practice several times weekly until you master the technique. Remember to establish your "peaceful place" trigger as instructed in the script. Notice that simple wording means more to the subconscious than good grammar.

I'm going to count backwards now from ten to one. As I do, it becomes easier and easier for me to imagine sights, sounds and feelings in my beautiful peaceful place . . .

Number Ten — deeper and deeper, relaxing physically . . . With each breath, it's easier to imagine my peaceful place . . .

Number Nine — deeper and deeper, relaxing mentally . . . With each sound, it's easier to imagine pleasant sights, sounds and feelings . . .

Number Eight — deeper and deeper, relaxing emotionally . . .

The deeper I go, the better I feel, and the deeper I want to go . . .

Number Seven — deeper and deeper, relaxing totally . . . The deeper I go, the easier it is to go even deeper, imagining my peaceful place . . .

Number Six — every nerve and muscle relaxes completely . . . as if I'm becoming a part of the peace that I imagine . . .

Number Five — each number making it easier and easier to go deeper and deeper . . . and it feels SO good to just relax . . .

Number Four — as I go deeper, it becomes easier and easier to imagine sights, sounds, and feelings that are so calm, and so peaceful . . .

Number Three — just drifting into total relaxation . . . into my place of total peace . . . where I can enjoy being anywhere I wish now . . .

Number Two — just relaxing at my ideal peaceful place now . . .

Number One — waaaaaaaaaaaaay down deep . . . Relaxing into a very deep, inner peace . . . a very deep, inner peace . . .

As I touch my finger to my thumb, or take a deep breath and think the word "relax," it's an automatic reminder of my inner peace. (Touch a finger to your thumb, and take a deep breath.) *Whenever I do this in the waking state, I feel calm and composed, free to think with a clear mind . . . but for now, I can just enjoy going even deeper into relaxation . . . deeper and deeper . . .*

With each breath I take, it's easier and easier to enjoy my freedom of imagination, to go to a favorite vacation spot now . . . and imagine my IDEAL vacation . . . doing what I enjoy doing, and relaxing as well . . .

In my mind, as much time as I wish can pass . . . and I feel as though I've enjoyed an hour's nap . . . I feel like I've enjoyed an hour's nap . . .

Before emerging from meditation, imagine feeling the way you wish to feel. Then, when ready, count forward from one to five and awaken yourself.

Most hypnotherapists use a similar method to help clients establish a peaceful place. The act of taking the deep breath (or touching your thumb and finger) WHILE imagining your peaceful place anchors a sense of inner peace to that act. Anchoring your peaceful place into your trigger during trance compares to programming your computer. Activating your trigger during the conscious state compares to pushing the "Execute" button on your computer. Your deep breath (and/or touching thumb and finger) will now become a trigger for *inner peace!*

**Reprinted from a portion of Chapter 8 of* Master the Power of Self-Hypnosis. *©1998 by C. Roy Hunter, all rights reserved. Published by Sterling Publishing.*

Once you learn the technique above, you may expand upon the mental imagery by rehearsing (in your imagination) the ability to successfully use your *peaceful place trigger*. Just like a singer rehearses before a performance, your rehearsals can take place in the safety and privacy of your own inner mind. Once somebody pushes your buttons, that's performance time! As any musician can tell you, several rehearsals improve your chances of a good performance.

If you prefer, you may record an audiotape for playback during your meditation. If you do, then change the first-person format to second-person format in the above script.

Enhancing the Program with Choices

Whenever our buttons get pushed, we have three healthy choices and one unhealthy choice.

The three healthy ones are: *now, later,* or *let it go*. The choice that is hazardous to our health and wealth is: *stuff it,* and pretend it does not bother us. Unfortunately, this hazardous option is often made in an effort to ignore our feelings and avoid revealing that someone penetrated our emotional defenses.

Many of us learned to stifle our feelings because well-intentioned parents taught us that children should be "seen and not heard" etc. It is my opinion that children and adults alike should learn *when and how* to properly express negative emotional feelings. As adults, we often stuff our emotions rather than risking a confrontation that might be a no-win situation. When negative emotions are stuffed, eventually the subconscious will find an outlet in one or more of various ways. Some people might take out their frustrations on family members, or by literally kicking the dog. Others can get sick or accident prone. Many cover their frustrations with addictions — sugar, alcohol, smoking, etc. While I believe in moderation, frustrated feelings can contribute to addictions — or other far more serious problems if repressed emotions erupt like a volcano at the wrong time and place. Now let's look at the healthy choices. They are explained in more detail in my hypnosis text, *The Art of Hypnosis* (3rd Edition, Kendall/Hunt Publishing, 2000).

Now

A wise king once wrote that there is a time and place for everything. There is a time and place for responding immediately when your buttons are pushed.

Certainly if a small child starts running towards the street, any loving parent would yell out, "No!" Most parents will correct a child immediately when the infraction occurs, even if only verbally. An employer will generally say something to an employee on the spot if he/she does something that needs to be addressed immediately. If a prospective customer offers an objection to a sales consultant, an immediate response creates a better probability of a sale. If a friend makes a cutting remark, you might reply in a manner appropriate for the circumstances and seek an immediate apology, explanation, or resolution.

Later

Some situations are better handled later, at a more appropriate time and place. Perhaps a friend embarrassed you in front of others, and you wish to confront the person in private in order to increase the chance of resolution. Perhaps a supervisor says something to an employee in private rather than in front of his or her peers. Perhaps you wish a second opinion before confronting somebody, or you may simply wish to "sleep on it." If you choose "later" as your choice, you must follow through — otherwise this choice automatically becomes the "stuff it" option.

Let it go

Occasionally, situations occur in which we have more to lose than we have to gain by expressing our discontent to someone. For example, a friend might simply be having a bad day, so we choose to ignore the desire to dish it back, and simply let it go. In business, an arrogant boss, or a difficult customer or client might push our buttons, but venting to that person might be costly professionally or financially. In such a case, without condoning the bad behavior, simply *release* the other person from the apology he/she used to owe you, and forgive yourself for buying into the negative emotions. (This may be done silently.) When I make this choice, I take a deep breath and think the word "release" as I let the air out of my lungs.

Making the choice

When someone pushes your buttons, use your peaceful place trigger, and immediately make a choice: *now, later,* or *let it go*. You have the power of choice, so you accept both the benefits and consequences of making your choice. Does this mean you will always make the best choice? Of course not, but we learn from our choices.

When you master the mental mini-vacation, rehearse your ability to make each of the three choices by fantasizing situations in which you would use each of the three healthy choices. By doing so in the safety of your imagination, you will be programming your inner mind to make a choice when you use your peaceful place trigger. Tell yourself that you make the best choice, according to your best wisdom, knowledge, understanding, training and experience.

Mastering the Technique

Generally, the more deeply you can relax (without falling asleep), the easier it is to more vividly use your imagination. Minor goals are easy to accomplish when you master the technique. However, for major goals, I personally find it helpful to have a hypnotherapist guiding me on my mental journey, even though I have taught and certified other professional hypnotherapists since 1987.

Self-hypnosis is like a mental muscle. While I can move a chair by myself, it is easier to move a couch if someone is lifting the other end. If you have a couch to move in your inner mind, choose a hypnotherapist to help you reprogram your subconscious.

Several years ago a realtor saw me professionally for assistance learning self-hypnosis. He tripled his income within one year after mastering the technique. Others who successfully utilize the mental mini-vacation have reported the ability to maintain greater self-control during times of stress, resulting in making wiser decisions. Managers have found their people-skills enhanced by their increased ability to remain calm. Sales people have increased their incomes by staying calm while overcoming objections. Some have enjoyed better family relationships at home. Which benefits might *you* enjoy by mastering this mental exercise?

Mastering this technique is an art — and no artist is perfect. Rather than striving for perfection, simply endeavor to be the best you can be. Often we try to be perfect under the guise of "professionalism" or because of past parental programming. Some days my best is better than other days because of how I feel physically, or because of other circumstances going on around me personally or professionally. We can control only ourselves, not others; but by being our best, we increase our ability to motivate others, when appropriate.

Life is about making choices and accepting responsibility for the choices we make. The primary benefit in the peaceful place trigger is that it reminds the inner mind to empower us to make better choices in life. Become the captain of your own mindship, and realize that you have the power to make it so.

ABOUT C. ROY HUNTER, M.S.

Roy Hunter, the published author of four books, was inducted into the International Hypnosis Hall of Fame in April of 2000 for his written contributions to the hypnotherapy profession. He is a respected trainer in his field, having taught advanced workshops on both sides of the ocean. He has taught professional hypnosis in a college since 1987, and is available for lectures and training in self-hypnosis, or professional hypnosis training.

Contact Information:
C. Roy Hunter, M.S.
E-mail: alliance@self-empowerment.tv.
Website: www.royhunter.com

CPR Training: How Balance Can Save Your Life

by Kevin Lust, CSP

If you sometimes feel you have too many people with too many demands piling on too much pressure to do too many things, you have too many "toos" in your life and it's time to set some of them aside. Though for years we've been lectured on the secrets of time management and of how to get more done, the real antidote to the pressure of doing too much might be getting more from what we already do. While Olympic medalists, Hall of Fame athletes, and *Fortune 500* CEO's often cite their unrelenting approach to their profession as a key to their success, many will say in private that their all-consuming drive has left their lives woefully lacking in some areas. Some people live life only for themselves and the often-fleeting pleasure they can find for the moment. A few will focus only on what they can do for others and lose themselves along the way. For all of us, balance in life — and across all areas of our lives — is the missing key to real happiness.

The ability to attend to the different areas of our lives often is absent in one-track-mind peak performers and also gets lost when the rest of us have to work too much overtime on our job, when the kids' schedules take over the entire family's calendar, or even when our own hobbies or habits take up more time than they should. To get back in balance and enjoy a truly successful life, we need to remember our CPR training. In this case, the acronym doesn't mean Cardio-Pulmonary Resuscitation, although that's a very good thing to know, but rather Career, Personal, and Relationships: the three main areas of our lives. If we can devote energy to each category, not only will we enhance that part of our lives, but we also will be able to claim a better life overall.

So how can we boost our performance in each of the three areas? Let's look at our careers first.

Zig Ziglar summed up the primary dilemma many people face regarding their work lives when he pointed out that too many of us spend most of our evenings worried about our next day's work and then all day at work worried about what's going on at home. "No wonder nothing ever gets done," Zig says, "nobody ever knows where they're at!" He's right. Competing demands for our time, attention, and energy often manifest themselves at exactly the wrong time: when we can do nothing about them. Whether that means we are at our child's soccer game when we think of that unreturned phone message from our biggest client, in the middle of helping a customer when it's time to go to lunch, or in a meeting with our boss when we remember the dog's veterinary appointment, our attention to the undoable leaves us unable to act where we can do something. We're ineffective at best, our stress level rises, and we may end up needing the other CPR.

To cure our wandering attention, we need a reminder to focus. Keep this phrase handy and repeat it to yourself when you feel your energies start to drift, especially at work.

Lust Lesson #1: Be where you are.

While this may seem to be the most obvious of obvious advice, don't let the simplicity of the words distract you from their value. How many times have you made a mistake, left something out, missed an opportunity, or otherwise dropped the ball, not because you were incapable of doing the right thing, but because your mind was on the wrong thing. Schoolteachers know not to save the most important lessons for the week before vacation, because they recognize that those lessons will never be heard, let alone learned. With spring break or summer recess dominating their young charges' thoughts, savvy instructors bow to the inevitable and make the last few days a review. Many of us never graduate. We spend our whole lives wishing we were somewhere else, hoping we were doing something different, or dreaming of the day when we don't have to do anything anymore.

To break that cycle and get the most value from what time we have, when you're at work, *be* at work. When you are playing with your children, *play* with your children. This lesson stands as particularly meaningful for anyone required to work beyond the boundaries of a normal workday. What if you stayed focused only on your work all day and got the job done? Think of how focused you are right before your big deadline or when the "big boss" is on the plant floor. What if you worked like that all the time? You might be able to go home once in a while!

One way to develop that kind of focus is to remember another key lesson.

Lust Lesson #2: Measure your success by results.

Too often, people impress themselves more with how busy they are than with what they accomplish. Don't let the busy-ness of your day get in the way of the business that needs to be done. Your to-do list can be one item long and still be valuable if what you cross off is what needs to be crossed off. Of course, you need to decide what belongs on the list.

And what belong on the list are those actions that provide the greatest value to you and your organization. Which of the activities on which you spend your time mean the most to the company's bottom line and to your paycheck? Accountants call it Return on Investment: how much will we get back compared to how much we put in. We can use the same formula to determine where to focus our attention, our actions, and our energy. We must be ruthless in assessing the value of every function and in casting aside all activity that does not produce value. Then, at the end of the day, we can decide whether we accomplished all that we wanted to or not.

Long-time St. Louis Cardinals baseball scout Jim Belz told of how many times he'd find himself on a dusty ball field in the small-town home of the latest high school phenom that his contacts would promote to him. Hearing of the prospect's marvelous feats, perhaps the kid's ability to pitch a baseball at 85 or 90 or even 95 miles an hour, Jim would schedule a visit and prepare to be impressed. Only to find that, on the day of the game, Jim's radar gun would measure the "can't-miss" kid's throws at 70 or 75 miles an hour. Not bad for a high-school player, but certainly not pro material. For all the hype and advance publicity, the young man just might not have what it takes to make the big leagues. And Jim would know it. "The gun doesn't lie," Jim would say. And he was right.

As hard as it was to judge these young men, Jim knew that was his job. They may have been fine examples of humanity — good students, involved citizens, and all-around good kids — but Jim knew that success in professional baseball would depend solely on how well they could do their job. For a baseball pitcher, although there are exceptions, success usually comes from throwing the ball fast. And if the scout's measuring stick says the pitch wasn't fast, if the radar gun reads "leisurely," the boy was not likely to be successful, no matter what anyone said about him.

You may say you were busy. (And most people look for any opportunity to say so.) You may have a to-do list twenty-two pages long. You may even convince yourself that you have worked hard. But at the end of your workday, how fast did you really throw the ball? What did you really accomplish? Were you just where you were supposed to be, doing what you were supposed to do? Or were you all the way there, creating measurable results that contributed to your success?

Define your results. Decide how to measure them. Keep track, and, above all, stay focused in order to build the career part of your life. With your work, the Career leg of our balancing act, on solid ground, we can work on building the Personal and the Relationship sides of our lives.

And it is that personal side of things that often suffers as our jobs and families demand so much. When everybody is yelling for something, your boss for more work, your kids for lost socks, your spouse for more attention, your goldfish for clean water, it is easy to forget yourself. You don't yell loud enough. And if you do yell at yourself, people look at you funny. So, how can we find a way to give ourselves the time we need for ourselves?

Actually, we have answered the question in how we asked it. *Find* a way. Most of what little time we have to ourselves is governed by routine. Think of how you get ready in the morning. Like most people, you probably follow a remarkably routine pattern for bathing, brushing your teeth, and eating your Pop-tarts. In fact, some people carry that routine into their cars in the morning. Even if you're not putting your make-up on in the rear-view mirror while driving, you no doubt are following exactly the same route to work every day. This mindless trip can be made without thinking and that allows us time to do what? We get to think about what's waiting for us at work or what we didn't get done at home! Which is precisely the problem we are defining.

With the few minutes of our day that we have to ourselves thus given to everyone else in our life, it's no wonder we feel short-changed. We're even thinking of others when we're in the shower. That's very compassionate, but hardly effective — or rejuvenating. So how can we break this pattern and take some time for ourselves? Here are two ways, among several others.

Lust Lesson #3: Get off the interstate.

Lust Lesson #4: Turn off the TV.

These two lessons go together and both are metaphorically larger than they are literally. Both can change your life.

The first change, getting off the interstate, means just that. Instead of following the common practice of choosing your route based on how wide a line is on a map, why not consider the best way to get there. And the widest line, the interstate, while typically faster, isn't always better. The four- and six- and twelve-lane speedways serve their purpose, and when you absolutely have to get somewhere in a hurry, take them. And say, "hi" to all the fast food joints for me on your way. But when you can schedule your trip for a calmer day, get off the main road. You'll be amazed at what you'll find and at how much fun you'll have.

When is the last time you enjoyed a cone from the walk-up window at a roadside ice cream stand or had a meal cooked by the person who's name is on the restaurant? No, not "Ronald;" think "Fritz's" or "Di's Place." Have you ever taken a moment to walk down the aisle at an antique store and to consider how much of your stuff at home actually qualifies? What about cows? Have you seen any cows lately? There are two cows for every five people in the United States. Do you know where yours are?

Don't take this too literally. You might not have a cow within a hundred miles of you, nor any raging desire to see one, but realize how much you miss by taking the same road all the time. Consider these signs from some roads less traveled:

On the gate to a farmer's field: "No trespassers. *Survivors* will be prosecuted.

On the signboard of a small-town church: "Honk if you love peace and quiet."

And from the window of a tiny deli in downtown Waukegan, Illinois: "Seating for 1000 — 18 at a time!"

This is not the sort of stuff you find on the interstate.

And don't miss the broader value of this lesson. We travel so fast through our lives that we never see many of the fun things that happen on the way. We're so eager for our kids to talk that we fail to appreciate their success in communicating without words. We're so anxious to buy our first house that we don't meet people in our apartment building who might stay friends long after we've moved away. We can't wait to get to Wally World on vacation, and we drive right past the World's Largest Ball of Twine. Okay, so missing that last one wouldn't be so bad, but we can pity parents who miss even one day of their child's life because they were wishing it already were the next day.

Getting wrapped up in getting there is what sends us to the interstate day after day and week after week, living only what we've already lived. Break your routine, find a new route, and start enjoying the drive. Thoreau said, "Many men go fishing all their lives without knowing it is not the fish they are after." Stop worrying about how many fish you caught and enjoy your time on the boat. This is the difference between a journey focus and destination focus.

While we're on the subject of changing habits, how about our good friend and constant companion: the television. This is the number one example of how routine spoils life. For too many people, the soundtrack of their own life has been drowned out by the laugh tracks of decades-old sit-coms. We can't start our day without our local station's "Wakin' Up Weather" and the same channel goes on when we get home from work for the early evening news. The rest of our night becomes a matter of "what's on?" instead of "what's going on?" And then we finish our day watching the same depressing news we saw when we got home or, if we can stay up a little longer, Leno or Letterman making jokes about the news we just watched. This is not an agenda for a fulfilling life.

Don't mistake this as an outright or complete rejection of television. You can find plenty of entertaining, educational, thrilling, or just plain old fun programs on TV. And you should. That is, you should when you've *decided* that you are going to watch TV. The problem is that most people let the TV decide. They turn on the tube and then, even if there is nothing particularly interesting showing, settle for whatever hurts the least to watch.

Beyond the harm experts cite of the influence of television in our lives (the repeated and dangerously influential viewing of murder, debauchery, and Anna Nichol Smith), the pain of habit again gets in the way. By using TV as an automatic companion, we miss opportunities to interact with the people with whom we should be making contact. Leave the TV off the next time you come home and watch what really happens instead. The things that fill that sudden, silent void might astound you. You actually may have a real conversation with your spouse or child (no guarantees on this one if your kids are teenagers). And, if no one else is around, you might feel an urge to call or write your parents or that college friend you haven't heard from since Christmas. You might decide to take a chair outside to enjoy a cool beverage and an evening out or retreat to your favorite corner inside with a book and a cup of hot chocolate.

The point is that something will take the place of whatever you would have watched on television. Once you have experienced that something (and be careful that it is not only the internet, which is virtually the same and just as addictive) you then have something to compare to the formerly automatic choice of turning on TV. Then you are able to make a conscious decision about the best use of the next few minutes or hours of your life.

This wonderful personal tip also provides you a powerful opportunity to enhance your relationships. Try leaving the radio off and unplugging the kids' video player for a few minutes the next time you go on a long car trip. If you can get past the routine "Are-we-there-yets?" you might enjoy a trip of remarkable relationship building with your family instead of returning home needing a vacation from your vacation.

This highlights another key challenge for us in our relationships. Too often the nagging questions or the petty annoyances are all we remember from our family trip. If we make it outside in the evening, all we see is the grass we expected our child to mow or the toys the little ones left out. We watch TV and see in some imaginary character, played by an actor who is not even remotely like that in real life, the person we wish our partner was, dwelling on all the things our partner is not. We see only what is bad and what we lack.

To break this spiral, and make no mistake, it only curls downward, remember an old Nigerian proverb that says, "We marry with only one eye." That's true, isn't it? During the time of courtship, whether that be in dating, applying for a job, or even deciding where to hang out, all we see are the good things about the person across from us. Our "good eye" is wide open and we see everything through the soft-focus lens of a forties romance movie. We enjoy our partner's every word, phrase, and sentence, and his or her personal habits are ever so cute and endearing. Think of the young person in love who hears "her cute little laugh," or loves "the way he nuzzles my neck when we're out." Within a few years (or even months — sometimes days), those passionate descriptions devolve into "her incessant cackle" or "he won't leave me alone!"

Pretty soon it seems that anyplace — or anyone — has to be better than here. Not only does our "bad eye" open, sometimes the "good eye" closes!

We create that problem for ourselves by focusing only on the things we wish were different. We grow angry about our wife's indecisiveness instead of revering her thoughtfulness. We lie awake frustrated by our husband's snoring instead of feeling comforted by his presence beside us. We constantly criticize our children's behavior instead of enjoying the little things they do well. Hey, at least they're potty-trained, right? That's real important by the time they get to college.

The counterpoint to developing a negative view of the people in our lives is to remember our "good eye."

Lust Lesson #5: Keep both eyes open.

When your relationship with your spouse starts to lose its fire, look for the things that sparked your interest in the first place. If those things aren't there any more (or are hidden by a few extra layers of life) find something that makes your partner interesting today. Don't pull in your driveway and get mad because of the bicycles strewn in your path without pausing to say thanks to the God who gave you children with healthy legs. Don't be disappointed in your brother for forgetting your birthday without reminding yourself that you can still beat him in golf. This doesn't mean you put on your rose-colored glasses and don't notice when behavior needs to change. You can still go in and turn off your kids' X-Box until they move their bikes. But it does mean you should balance your negative view of what people aren't with the very, very good they often are.

While it may seem contradictory, expanding our commitment to more areas of our lives actually can improve our performance in each area. Rather than define a driven, full-bore, no-distractions approach to our career as the key to success in business, we seek an approach that allows us time to recuperate and enjoy the time we spend with others. Rather than lead a self-centered existence, we promote individuals who make a real contribution in the workplace and who appreciate the value of others. Rather than allow relationships to drive us to distraction, we look for how to make the best of the people we are lucky enough to have in our lives, at work and at home.

So, the key to success in life is to make each part of our life successful. With our excellent CPR training, we do more than save lives; we enjoy life as well.

About Kevin Lust, CSP

Kevin Lust, CSP, makes people's work more effective and their lives a little easier. Though fifteen years of research in what works better at work and what is more fun at play, Kevin has become an expert in "productivity with passion" and he has taught tens of thousands of people his inspiring "Lust Lessons" in over 1,600 professional presentations in 16 countries on four continents.

A blue-collar background and a banking career give Kevin the grounding he needs to bring insights and answers to organizations and individuals striving to become better at leadership, management, communication, balance, and even integrity. He is the Founder and President of Lust Development Group, Inc., and General Partner of Smith-Miner Productions. Kevin has authored two audio programs, authored or co-authored three books and is a Preferred Pretzel Patron at Auntie Anne's Pretzel Shoppes.

Contact Information:
Kevin Lust, CSP
Lust Development Group, Inc.
#349; 2745 South Sixth Street
Springfield, IL 62703-4071
Phone: (217) 241-5877
Toll-free: (888) 241-5878
Fax (217) 241-5879
E-mail: kevinlust@kevinlust.com
Website: www.kevinlust.com

Be Yourself

by Doug Smart, CSP

"The function of education is to help you from childhood not to imitate anybody, but be yourself all the time."
— Jiddu Krishnamurti

Trying to be someone you are not consumes lots of energy. My friend, Max Howard, has been a professional actor for over 35 years. He knows playing a role can be exhausting. "Acting is illusion," Max has said. "To perform in such a way that an audience can accept the illusion that a character is authentic takes a lot of energy. The farther a character's personality is from one's own, the more resources it demands. Performing can be fun but it is rarely as easy as it seems, even when you have played the part for many performances."

One reason some people feel out of balance is they pretend to be people they are not. They play roles that are not comfortable fits. Some salespeople who are reserved by nature think they need to be boisterous and animated to impress potential clients. Some managers who are deferential by nature feel they need to bark orders in order to gain the respect of the people they manage. They act inauthentically. The result is they feel the stress of being out of balance and the people they are trying to impress are left wondering what the act is all about.

Brian, a salesman for a large convention hotel, is an analytical thinker who is naturally good at structuring projects, organizing details, and following through with promises. His manner is conservative, factual, and low key. His repeat customers appreciate his reliability, and several book his hotel for their important meetings year after year because of the comfort and trust they feel knowing he will handle the details according to his personal high standards. Brian prefers to work alone rather than in a group setting, but he constantly tells himself he should loosen up and be more outgoing and spontaneous like the other salespeople. He told me he has a running dialog in his mind telling himself he should get better at telling jokes and making small talk "like a salesperson is supposed to," although he feels such behavior is petty at best and manipulative at worst. When prospective customers visit his hotel on fact-finding trips he knows many of them want to enjoy being dazzled with food and entertainment. He plays along — he has even memorized a few jokes — but does not much enjoy participating. He describes it as a necessary evil of his job. He has learned to smile a lot, even when he does not feel like smiling. In a good-natured way, Brian's boss ribs him about being an old man before his time. Brian is thinking of working at a different hotel.

Susan has a terrific sense of humor and says she is a whiz at managing a household of three boys (ages 7 to 15), a husband and two large dogs. At home she has clear objectives about what she sees needs to be accomplished and is pretty good at making plans and getting things done. On Saturdays when she chauffeurs her children to soccer games, doctor appointments, and other destinations she has her route mapped out, she says, "as tightly as a four-hour tour of Europe." Her house is generally neat and every member has specific duties. Her kids lovingly call her "General Mom." But her work life is a different matter. Although her friends on the job know she has strong opinions, Susan tends to be quiet at meetings and deferential to those with seniority. She is familiar with the Japanese expression, "The nail that sticks up gets hammered down." Behind the scenes she allows herself to be freer in expressing herself openly to co-workers. Not exactly a shrinking violet, she is, however, more likely to be seen as a follower than a leader, especially since she is not in a managerial position. She says her job is just a job. She would like to have more challenging and interesting work. Every day she leaves for home promptly at 5:00, feeling tired.

At work, Brian and Susan have modified their natural behaviors to be more like they think they should be. Neither of them is happy with the results.

All of us have to adapt to our environments. Think of it as similar to a woman who puts on makeup to enhance the best features of her face. There might be a bit of covering a blemish or a few lines, but basically she is highlighting her best features. The amount of energy that goes into the process is low and the results are gratifying. This is different from a woman who applies heavy makeup to obliterate her face so she can craft a new one. That takes a lot of work and, no matter how beautifully done, the results are inauthentic, phony, and short-term. The people who see her cannot help but wonder what she looks like underneath the goo.

It would be easy to advise them to quit their jobs and seek better-suited employment elsewhere. But neither wants to do that. They have a lot invested in their jobs — years of on-the-job training, good friendships, and work that in itself is satisfying. So how can they find more balance in their lives? The answer lies in being true to themselves.

There are Four Behavioral Styles

Research indicates there are four main personality styles. Which of these sounds the most like you?

Direct, results-oriented, prefers to be in control, does not shy away from confrontation, sometimes forceful

Influential, outgoing, optimistic, fun-loving, expressive, spontaneous, dramatic, tends to be disorganized

Steady, patient, loyal, amiable, slow to change, values close relationships and calm surroundings, tends to be "low key"

Conscientious, conservative, reserved, finds peace in following rules, relies mainly on facts not emotions when making decisions

In different situations, each of us can be any of the above. However, nearly everyone tends naturally to favor one style more than the others. William Marston, a Harvard-educated Ph.D., published a book, *Emotions of Normal People*, that fueled research in this area and led to the acronym DISC to describe people whose behavior is predominately D (direct), I (influential), S (steady), or C (conscientious).

How to Find Your True Self

Probably, there have been times when you have made yourself to be more out-going or to take risks in trying new things. This is common, for example, at the start of a new job when we want very much to make a good impression on our new coworkers. And there have probably been times you have forced yourself to "settle down," as my Mom used to implore us kids, and be a patient listener or more attuned to the details of the project upon which you work. We make conscious behavioral adjustments that fit the situation at hand.

To find your true self, make a list of one hundred actions you take that make you feel happy. You can make your list over the course of a few days. Your items may be things such as leading a particular project team or quietly working alone on a project, reading business magazines or romance novels, taking new classes or watching reruns on television. To be sure, you will have items that fit each of the D, I, S, and C categories above. That is expected because you are a complex individual and to different degrees you are all four. However, you will see patterns that clearly indicate you are one (possibly two) of the D, I S, or C. This will help you see your natural behavioral style. And you will find the investment in time and mental energy will pay you back with a lifetime of understanding the combination of behaviors that give you happiness and ultimately a peaceful feeling of balance.

Let's take a close look at each of the four behavioral styles.

Primarily a D

D people tend to be assertive and task-focused. They have a sense of "I know what I want and I go after it." They are willing to take risks and like immediate results. They question authority. They like challenges and will take difficult assignments. Frequently competitive, they work or play to win. They are seen as "doers," "bottom line" thinkers, and as strong-willed. They are comfortable assuming leadership roles. Naturally fast paced, they make decisions quickly. They are goal-oriented and usually organized.

Control, power and authority motivate these people. Prestige is important, though they may pretend it is not. They resist being overly managed, controlled or supervised. They feel they are independent thinkers. They value efficiency although they like new activities. They tend to be traditional in the sense that once they master a way to do something effectively, they resist changing how they do it. To them, small talk tends to be a waste of time and emotional people can appear to be unfocused. Facts are more important than feelings although they do not like to get too deep into minute details. They have little patience for time-wasters, laziness or emotional displays.

Examples of well known D people are Hillary Clinton, Donald Trump, and Lucy from the Peanuts comics.

Primarily an I

I people tend to be shaped by their environment by influencing or persuading others. More than just meeting people, they enjoy making new friends. They tend to be outgoing and personable. Generally, they are articulate — but prone to exaggeration — and openly express their feelings. They are optimistic by nature and enjoy the company of enthusiastic, positive people. They tend to speak at a faster pace than others and smile readily, especially when trying to gain agreement. Not loners, I people prefer to work in groups or teams. More than the other three behavioral styles, "I's" are willing to trust others and believe in the likelihood of positive outcomes. They enjoy exploring new ideas and frequently initiate change. They have a penchant for self-improvement.

Social recognition and popularity motivate these people. Being the center of attention is considered a worthwhile place to be. They value public recognition and free expression. Having fun is an important and motivating component in work and relationships. They are seen as spontaneous, adventuresome and with a flair for the dramatic. They seek approval from others and enjoy friendly, casual and warm relationships. They tend to not be good time-managers and, unless they have a high D or S component, have difficulty staying organized. Emotional arguments carry weight with I people and can be more persuasive than facts. Decision-making based on gut-feelings, hunches, and intuition are considered valid and reliable.

Examples of well known I people are Bill Clinton and Snoopy

from the Peanuts comics.

Primarily an S

S people tend to seek cooperation of others in order to get the job done. They are most comfortable when they know what others expect of them and know how to get done what they need to do. They are slow to change and can be expected to conduct themselves in a consistent, predictable manner. As a rule they are patient, demonstrate loyalty, and especially value close relationships. They care about the feelings and needs of others to the point they will readily put the needs of others ahead of their own. Loving by nature, they like to belong to groups of similar-minded people. They dislike conflict and will avoid it when possible. They strive to foster harmony and understanding in group situations at work and home. They have a calming and comforting influence. They demonstrate good listening skills. Often they are seen as peacemakers. In a broad sense they are seen as the glue that holds society together.

Though they are emotional people, they tend to hold their own emotions inside unless provoked to anger or joy. They tend to have systematic approaches to getting work done and have an affinity for developing specialized skills. They value details. Often, they make decisions slowly, weighing the impact of potential outcomes against the needs of others. Maintaining the status-quo is desirable to S people, unless given compelling reasons for change. They find comfort in predictability. They are motivated by sincere appreciation and close friendships. They dislike insincerity and insensitiveness. They tend to focus on the "people side" of change, such as how a change could positively or negatively impact others. They prefer to keep a sharp distinction between their work and home lives.

Examples of well known S people are Ronald Reagan, Jimmy Carter, Barbara Bush, and Charlie Brown from the Peanuts comics.

Primarily a C

C people tend to be analytical, practical, and thorough by nature. They are more likely to follow or comply with rules than to make them. They hold themselves and others to high standards and experience frustration or disappointment when things don't work out "as they are supposed to." They are risk avoiders. They are especially uncomfortable making mistakes and can invest considerable time and energy gathering information or doing research before making a decision. They do not like to be rushed when making decisions. Quality and accuracy are what they seek. The abilities to organize information and track details are heightened in them. They usually prefer to work alone or in small teams and can be seen as reserved, passive and even withdrawn. Owning to their high standards, others can see them as perfectionists.

C people place more value on facts than on emotions. They have little patience for people who are "fakes" or overtly manipulative. Though they can be argumentative, they generally deal with conflict using subtle or indirect approaches. They prefer systematic approaches to handling routine situations. They are motivated by clearly defined performance expectations and the opportunity to demonstrate their expertise.

Examples of C people are George W. Bush, George Bush, and Linus from the Peanuts comics.

Benefits to Being Yourself

Each of us is unique. Each is a bundle of hopes, dreams, talents, and experiences that is as one-of-a-kind as fingerprints or DNA. Out of six billion people on the planet, no two have the same accumulation of knowledge and life lessons so no two people share a totally identical perspective. Yet, many of us put a tremendous amount of energy into trying to be like other people. Some people wish they were more ambitious. Some want to be more outgoing. Some fret over why they cannot enjoy a steady, drama-free life. And others work hard at developing their analytical skills, but they never seem to get as good as they feel they are expected to be. It takes a lot of energy, but ultimately the effort is as ineffective as a cat trying to be a dog.

I believe that within each of us lives three people: 1. The person we really are. 2. The person we think we ought to be. 3. The person we think that other people think we ought to be. To live a life of balance it is critical to nurture our true behaviors. You can do this by understanding your natural behavioral style and working with it, not against it. Shakespeare said, "This above all; to thine own self be true." Develop your natural strengths. Understand and compensate for your natural weaknesses. Be very good at being you. This may sound like stating the obvious, but some people have disdain for their natural behaviors as somehow inferior. They feel they would be better, more effective, perhaps more loved people, if they were more like someone else. If you find yourself agonizing that you "need to be more like _____," it is smart to pause and ask yourself, "Instead of trying to be like ___, what is it about me that I can develop further to help me be more effective?" Marsha Sinetar wrote a book titled, *Do What You Love, The Money Will Follow.* In it she advised that readers find balance and happiness by adjusting their lives to fit their natural behaviors, rather than wrestling to make their natural behaviors fit their circumstances.

Birds are born with instincts that guide them to successfully build nests appropriate to their species. They do not get nest building instructions from TV, magazines or training videos. They just know what to do. Through experience, and perhaps observation, they hone their nest building skills. To build your life, you have within you a set of innate behaviors. Through experience and observation you hone them. However, unlike birds, you also have the benefit of a discerning mind that allows you to seek information to help you grow your attitudes and skills for successfully being the best you possible. By working with, not against, your natural behaviors you will experience a greater feeling of balance. Be yourself.

ABOUT DOUG SMART, CSP

Doug Smart, CSP, is a successful business owner and a former top salesperson who is authoritative and authentic. He is a consultant, keynoter, trainer, and radio show host who has spoken at over 1,000 conventions, conferences, seminars, sales rallies and management retreats. Doug is the author or co-author Magnetic Leadership, How Real People Really Get Things Done at Work, *and* Fantastic Customer Service Inside & Out. *In 1998 the National Speakers Association awarded him the prestigious Certified Speaking Professional designation, their highest certification. Contact Doug's office for an information kit on bringing The Get Smart Series to your organization.*

Contact information:
Doug Smart, CSP
Smart Business, Inc.
P.O. Box 768024
Roswell, GA 30076
Phone: (770) 587-9784
E-mail: Doug@DougSmart.com
Website: www.DougSmart.com

RESOURCE LISTING

Alan Boyer
The Leader's Perspective
6 Pemford Place
Liberty, MO 64068
Phone: (816) 916-6141
Fax: (816) 781-4312
E-mail: AlanBoyer@leaders-perspective.com
Website: www.leaders-perspective.com

Peggy Farmer, Ph.D.
Self Mastery International
373 Landrum Road
Tryon, NC 28782
Phone: (828) 863-4681
E-mail: pfarmer@teleplex.net
Website: www.selfmasteryintl.com

Valla Dana Fotiades, M.Ed.
Energize Your Life!
P.O. Box 133
Waverly, FL 33877-0133
Phone: (863) 875-0759
Fax: (863) 324-7558
E-mail: Valladana@cs.com

C. Roy Hunter, M.S.
E-mail: alliance@self-empowerment.tv.
Website: www.royhunter.com

Kevin Lust, CSP
Lust Development Group, Inc.
#349; 2745 South Sixth Street
Springfield, IL 62703-4071
Phone: (217) 241-5877
Toll-free: (888) 241-5878
Fax: (217) 241-5879
E-mail: kevinlust@kevinlust.com
Website: www.kevinlust.com

David Mee-Lee, M.D.
4228 Boxelder Place
Davis, CA 95616
Phone: (530) 753-4300
Fax: (530) 753-7500
E-mail: info@dmlmd.com
Website: www.DMLMD.com

Laurie Santulli
Sound Decisions Consulting, Inc.
P.O. Box 270996
Tampa, FL 33688-0996
Phone: (813) 908-0000
Fax: (813) 908-1460
E-mail: LSantul@tampabay.rr.com
Website: www.sounddecisions.net

Doug Smart, CSP
Smart Business, Inc.
P.O. Box 768024
Roswell, GA 30076
Phone: (770) 587-9784
Fax: (770) 587-1050
E-mail: Doug@DougSmart.com
Website: www.DougSmart.com

Karen Ussery
Organized for Success
56 West Windsor Ave.
Phoenix, AZ 85003
Phone: (602) 248-2884
Fax: (602) 266-2101
Website: www.organizedforsuccess.com

Michelle M. Weil, Ph.D.
Human-Ware, LLC
Phone: (760) 730-3894
E-mail: Weil@Human-Ware.com
Website: www.Human-Ware.com

Patti Wood, M.A., CSP
2312 Hunting Valley Drive
Decatur, GA 30033
Phone: (404) 371-8228
E-mail: Pattiwood@PattiWood.com
Website: www.PattiWood.com
www.TheBodyLanguageLady.com

Ann Wright
The Wright Solutions
4321 Wakonda Drive
Norwalk IA 50211
Phone (515) 285-8154
E-mail: Wrightsolutions@juno.com